TIME'S DISTRACTIONS
A Play from the Time of Charles I

TIME'S DISTRACTIONS

A Play from the Time of Charles I

Edited by

DIANE WELTNER STROMMER

TEXAS A&M UNIVERSITY PRESS
College Station

Library of Congress Cataloging in Publication Data

Time's distractions.
    Time's distractions: a play from the time of Charles I.

    Variously attributed to M. Fane, Earl of Westmor-
land, and G. Chapman.
    "Exists in a single manuscript in British Museum,
MS. Egerton 1994."
    Bibliography: p.
    I. Strommer, Diane Weltner, 1935–
II. Westmorland, Mildmay Fane, Earl of, 1601–1666.
III. Chapman, George, 1559?–1634.
PR3291.A1T55   822'.4   75–43623
ISBN 0–89096–008–9

Manufactured in the United States of America
First edition

For my husband John and my brother Peter

Contents

Acknowledgments : ix

Introduction : 3

Time's Distractions : 47

Explanatory Notes : 93

Appendix: *Byron's Tragedy,* Act II : 111

References : 116

Acknowledgments

ALTHOUGH it has been a number of years since I was their student, for their superb teaching and for their love of drama I am grateful to have had the opportunity to study with Professors Emeriti Harold R. Walley and John Harold Wilson and Professor John B. Gabel of The Ohio State University. I am particularly indebted to Professor Gabel, who in suggesting this project to me gave up one of his own.

For their encouragement, love, and flexibility, my greatest debt is to my family, especially to my husband and to my children, Jae and Erik.

TIME'S DISTRACTIONS
A Play from the Time of Charles I

Introduction

MANY of the playwrights born in Elizabeth's reign died during the fourth decade of the seventeenth century: Chapman, Dekker, Jonson, Marston. Ford and Massinger lived until 1640, after which only Shirley remained. The great half-century of drama which began with Marlowe had come to an end. Dramatic activity steadily dwindled in the early 1640's, and by 1644 theatrical production seems to have virtually stopped; of two new plays that year, only one was performed. Of twenty-two new plays in 1641, between twelve and seventeen were acted; in 1642 only two of seven were performed; and in 1643, of the five recorded new plays, only a puppet show is certain to have had an audience.[1]

After a summer of sporadic fighting throughout England, the Civil War officially began on August 22, 1642. On September 2 Parliament passed a resolution which closed the theatres,[2] an act which is said to have killed the already dying drama. Not until the return of the monarchy in 1660 was the drama resurrected; hence, the period between 1642 and 1660 is seen as a hiatus in English dramatic history. This view, though certainly not a totally inaccurate one, has, however, been challenged in recent

[1] Alfred Harbage and S. Schoenbaum, *Annals of English Drama, 975–1700*, pp. 142–145.

[2] "Whereas publike Sports doe not well agree with publike Calamities, nor publike stage-plays with the Seasons of Humiliation, this being an Exercise of sad and pious solemnity, and the other being Spectacles of pleasure, too commonly expressing lascivious Mirth and Levitie: It is therefore thought fit, and ordeined by the Lords and Commons in this Parliament assembled, that while these sad Causes and set times of Humiliation doe continue, publike-Stage-playes shall cease, and be forborne." Alfred Harbage, *Cavalier Drama*, p. 177.

years. Leslie Hotson, for one, has turned up considerable evidence of surreptitious professional and amateur productions even in 1643. The suspicion grows that plays continued to be written and performed, but they were more frequently, though not exclusively, the works of Cavaliers for private halls than of professional playwrights for public theatres and more often in the countryside than in London. Because acting companies were split up and actors scattered, and because performances were illegal, records are few and often amount to no more than a tantalizing "to a playe and other foleyes" in a diary.[3] Any surviving play of this period has, therefore, some interest, if only for the glimpses it can provide into what is virtually a dark age in dramatic history.

One of the few such survivors is *Time's Distractions*. Anonymous and titleless, it exists in a single manuscript in British Museum MS. Egerton 1994. Below the *"Nomina Actorum"* appears the date "August 5th 1643" (fol. 212), a date which is probably close to the date of composition.[4] The play has been variously titled by its readers—*Time's Triumph, Juno in Arcadia, Juno's Pastoral,* or *The Bonds of Peace, Sight and Search*—but since I feel that none of these is particularly apt and that the first and last are actually misleading, I have retitled it *Time's Distractions,* a title which points to the central action of the play and which makes use of a phrase ubiquitous in contemporary popular literature.

Classified as a "masque" (Bullen), as an "allegorical show" (Bentley), and as a "pastoral-allegorical entertainment" (Harbage), the play has interesting connections both with some of the most popular genres of the Caroline period and with the political turmoil of the early 1640's. While it is certainly no masterpiece, *Time's Distractions* is less clumsy dramatically and theatrically than many contemporary plays, including several others in Egerton 1994 which have received more critical attention and are now in published editions. Since the play is for the most part the-

[3] Leslie Hotson, *The Commonwealth and Restoration Stage*, p. 17.
[4] See below, pp. 7–10.

4

atrically adept and carefully conceived and has several passages of genuinely fine verse, it is rather strange that it has received so little attention. Except for an unpublished edition done in 1950 as a University of Birmingham thesis by R. C. Elslay, an edition which is virtually inaccessible to American scholars,[5] the play has been the focus of only one article[6] and an item of incidental mention in several others. The folio in which it appears has, however, attracted interest.

The play is the tenth piece in MS. Egerton 1994, a folio volume of 349 leaves containing fifteen plays. Arthur Henry Bullen first drew attention to the importance of the folio in the appendix to the second volume of his *Collection of Old English Plays* (1883) and edited several of its plays for later volumes. The manuscript was purchased by the museum at the sale of Lord Charlemont's library on August 6, 1865. Nothing is known of the history of the manuscript before that date, but Bullen offers an interesting theory, which F. S. Boas has more recently supported. Bullen's contemporary, Sir George Warner, who cataloged the Dulwich Collection at the British Museum, thought that the folio had belonged to Dulwich College in London, which had in turn received it as a bequest from the actor William Cartwright, Jr., at the end of the seventeenth century. The conjecture is that Lord Charlemont borrowed the volume from his friend Edmund Malone, who had many of the Dulwich documents in his possession for years. "Mr. Warner's theory," Bullen concludes, "is that Malone lent the volume to Lord Charlemont, and that it was never returned." Bullen himself poses one obvious objection to the theory: "How came so acute a scholar as Malone to fail to draw attention to a Collection of such considerable interest?"[7] That question must remain unanswered. In support of Bullen's theory F. S. Boas has found that a number of the actors named in several of the plays in the folio flourished in the third and fourth decades of the seventeenth

[5] The waiting period for it currently is at least a year.
[6] J. D. Jump, "The Anonymous Masque in MS Egerton 1994," *Review of English Studies* 2 (April, 1935): 186–191.
[7] Arthur Henry Bullen, *A Collection of Old English Plays*, II, 418.

5

century and were associated with the William Cartwrights, father and son. Both were members of the Revels Company before the Civil War, and during it William Cartwright, Jr., became a bookseller and publisher. It was probably then that he began to collect play manuscripts, some of which he did, indeed, leave to Dulwich College. After the Restoration, Cartwright returned to acting and joined the King's Players at Drury Lane. Slight as I believe the evidence to be, there is, then, some logical, if not factual, basis for the conjecture that MS. Egerton 1994 moved from Cartwright to Dulwich College to Malone and finally to Charlemont. Boas believes this to be an accurate account of the folio's history and argues, further, that it was once part of the repertory of the Revels Company or of one of the other companies, a collection of plays which the theatrical upheaval during the Civil War or the fusion of the old companies after the Restoration could have brought into William Cartwright's hands.[8]

Attempts have also been made to discover the author of *Time's Distractions*. In an article and later in his book *Cavalier Drama*, Professor Alfred Harbage quite plausibly suggests Mildmay Fane, Earl of Westmorland, as the author of the play.[9] Fane's editor, Clifford Leech, finds Harbage's guess "intriguing" but concludes that although it is not impossible that Fane was the author, the evidence does not warrant including the work in the Westmorland canon, and that the play is "indeed a little too skillfully handled for Fane."[10] I find Fane to be much clumsier with theatrical detail and dramatic construction than the author of *Time's Distractions* and on this basis agree with Professor Leech's conclusion. I suspect that the similarities between *Time's Distractions* and Fane's work arise more from shared literary and dramatic conventions of their time than from common authorship.

[8] F. S. Boas, *Shakespeare and the Universities and Other Studies in Elizabethan Drama*, pp. 96–110.

[9] "An Unnoted Caroline Dramatist," *Studies in Philology* 31 (1934): 28–36, and *Cavalier Drama*, p. 201.

[10] Mildmay Fane, Earl of Westmorland, *Mildmay Fane's "Raguaillo D'Oceano," 1640, and "Candy Restored," 1641*, ed. Clifford Leech, p. 22.

Bullen was also the first to notice that a long passage in the play (ll. 215–252) is derived from the masque in Chapman's *Byron's Tragedy*. In a 1935 article in *Review of English Studies*, J. D. Jump also notes the relationship between the two passages and cites a number of additional lines and phrases which he believes to be taken from various works by Chapman. Jump further finds that "the anonymous author's fondness for puns and verbal jingles, and his habit of using rime to emphasize an important aphorism are also characteristic of Chapman" and, therefore, concludes that "it is evident that the piece is either the revision by an unknown hand of a masque by Chapman, or a work, substantially original, containing important borrowings from the earlier poet." The triviality of some of the resemblances inclines Jump to the former conjecture because "it is difficult to imagine a dramatist deliberately stealing single phrases of no particular note."[11] Most of the parallels Jump cites are, however, common figures, as common as are punning and rhyming for emphasis, which occur in the work of almost every seventeenth-century playwright. The conjecture that *Time's Distractions* is the revision of a lost masque by Chapman is unwarranted; no real evidence exists to support it, and much argues against it. The more interesting connection between the two is that the unknown playwright was attracted to the masque scene from *Byron's Tragedy* and enlarged upon it for his own play, a matter to be discussed later.

Dating

Although I do not believe the manuscript to be an autograph,[12] internal evidence strongly suggests that the date of August 5, 1643, written below the *"Nomina Actorum,"* is quite close to the date of actual composition. It is likely that the play was written no earlier than the preceding year.

Part of the evidence for this dating derives from the political hints in the play's action and from England's social and political

[11] Jump, "The Anonymous Masque," pp. 190, 191.
[12] See below, p. 45.

7

turmoil. The struggle between Crown and Parliament rapidly reached a crisis in 1642. Charles and his queen fled from Whitehall on the night of January 10, and the opposing positions grew more rigid that winter and spring. By summer, sporadic fighting had broken out throughout the land. On August 22, 1642, when Charles raised his standard at Nottingham, the Civil War officially began. References in the play to "unnatural strife and bloody wars" (l. 115), the wartime problems of unpaid, wounded soldiers (ll. 115–157), poverty-stricken Anglican priests (ll. 158–160), the proliferation of newspapers and pamphlets (l. 882), and the play's concluding hope for a "future peace" (l. 1008) all suggest that *Time's Distractions* was written after the beginning of the war, between September, 1642, and August, 1643. The popular songs in the play, the fashions referred to, and even its proverbs generally support this date; however, since these indexes of popular taste were current for a decade or much longer, it is impossible to date the work precisely by them.

The strongest case for the date rests on the repetition and significance of the term *distractions* in the play and on the purgation of Time in act 5 of "libels," "diurnals," and "weekly intelligences." In a speech in 1642 Charles I expressed his desire "to settle the Peace of the Kingdom, and compose the present Distractions,"[13] and in contemporary accounts of the events of 1642 and 1643 the term is ubiquitous. The *Oxford English Dictionary* cites the king's speech as the first occurrence of the word in its senses of "disorder or confusion of affairs, caused by internal conflict or dissension" and of "a community torn by dissension or conflict of parties"; even if his were not the first usage of the term to describe England's political situation, it certainly must have helped to give that sense currency. In the play, the word *distraction* appears five times, often with its additional meaning of temporary madness, and the action of the play focuses on Time's distractions, which change the nature of the Arcadian world. It is

[13] Edward, Earl of Clarendon, *The History of the Rebellion and Civil Wars in England,* ed. W. Dunn Macray, V, 386.

"distraction" which Envy determines "to infuse" into Time, "distractions" from which Arcadia suffers, and "distractions" from which it is finally relieved by Juno.[14] The playwright appears to be deliberately emphasizing a term which referred to current political dissension, a condition perceived by many writers on both sides of the conflict in the early 1640's as madness and upheaval in their world order.

Similarly topical were the complaints about libels and newspapers, which the play alludes to as "barking libels" (l. 847) and "diurnals and weekly intelligences" (l. 882). The abolition of the Star Chamber court by Parliament late in 1641 effectively ended censorship and relieved printers of the fear of prosecution for publishing rash political pamphlets. From that time and for some time thereafter cheap newspapers of every political cast were published, 722 of them by 1645. By the end of November, 1641, an enterprising printer began issuing a small quarto pamphlet every seven days which summarized the events of the preceding week in Parliament. Within a few weeks rival journals appeared: "They warned their readers against each other, claiming that one only was authentic, the rest vile counterfeits. But soon they gave up warning the public and wooed it instead—offering as time went on more news, prettier headings, woodcut decorations, shorter and more attractive titles: *Diurnal Occurrences, True Diurnal Occurrences,* and in time a whole flight of *Mercuries.*"[15] Officially, Parliament disapproved of them, but since the early newspapers gave only its point of view and so suited Parliament's political purposes, for several years no action was taken to prevent their publication. Eventually the Royalists, too, would use this potent weapon, but initially they had only the harshest words for the outpourings of the press, which was "at liberty for the publishing [of] the most invective, seditious, and scurrilous pamphlets that their wit and malice could invent."[16] The *OED* gives

---

[14] See lines 381, 565, 585, 838, 1003.
[15] Cicely Veronica Wedgwood, *The King's War,* pp. 37–38. See also Clarendon, *History of the Rebellion,* I, 263–264.
[16] Clarendon, *History of the Rebellion,* I, 187.

1640 as the first appearance of the term *diurnals* in the sense of a newspaper published at periodical intervals, but it was after their proliferation in 1641–1642 that the word came into general currency.[17]

The history of the term *weekly intelligences* closely parallels that of *diurnals*; the *OED* cites 1641 as the first occurrence of its use with the meaning of "newspaper": "R. BRATHWAIT (*title*) Mercurius Britannicus: or, the English Intelligencer." Other authorities give 1643 as the date of its first appearance, which, is of course, inaccurate, but again suggests that it did not have frequent use immediately.[18]

The temporary end of the censorship laws and the tension of the political conflict also explain the increasing contemporary references to libels. As Clarendon complains, they appeared everywhere: "Cheap senseless libels were scattered about the city, and fixed upon gates and public remarkable places, traducing some, and proscribing others, of those who were in highest trust and employment."[19] In act 5 of *Time's Distractions* when Time is purged, Love comments that "his belching stomach's full of barking libels" (1. 847) and that "he farts diurnals and weekly intelligences" (1. 882), unlikely ailments before 1641.

The evidence suggests, then, 1641 as the earliest date of composition and August 5, 1643, as the latest. Because of topical allusions which can safely be connected with the Civil War and wartime conditions in England, I am inclined to date the play after the outbreak of the Civil War. It is also possible that the "swearing oaths and lies of all kinds and colors" (1. 881) of which Time is purged refer obliquely to the Oath of Covenant introduced on June 6, 1643, by the war faction in Parliament in order to strengthen its position. The reference is, however, too cryptic to yield to the temptation to narrow the date of composition.

[17] See Wedgwood, *The King's War*, pp. 37ff., and F. S. Siebert, *Freedom of the Press in England, 1476–1776*, pp. 191, 203.
[18] See Jump, "The Anonymous Masque," p. 191, and footnote 17.
[19] Clarendon, *History of the Rebellion*, I, 263–264.

10

The Political Background

While the crisis of the reign of Charles I was in substance a struggle for power between the Crown and Parliament, it is an oversimplification to make of it a rigid dichotomy between Royalists and Parliamentarians, between Anglicans and Puritans, or between Cavaliers and Roundheads. Like most political crises, this one bred men of all political complexions, few of whom wanted war. Most men reluctantly gave up their hope for compromise between the leaders of both sides, for without compromise the future looked somber. By the time of the Grand Remonstrance in 1642, however, many men believed Parliament had begun to unleash forces which would rend the fabric of society. The fear of a permanent perversion of the world they had known began to outweigh religious concerns. Those who became Royalists, even reluctant ones, were agreed that to recognize the right of rebellion for any cause would be to make stable government impossible. Rebellion, they argued, could not be confined; it would produce civil war which, evil in itself, would tend to jettison the legal basis of society and ultimately destroy all order. No matter what reservations they may once have had about Laud and Strafford's authoritarianism, about Queen Henrietta Maria's Catholicism, or about Charles himself, Royalists were one on this issue. "They were united," says one historian, "by a sense of danger, not only to the constitution as they conceived it, but to the rule of law and to the whole social order and all the traditions of England that many, at least, of them sincerely loved."[20]

Whether their primary concerns were spiritual or material, political or social, Royalists discerned England's being wrenched away from the values which had led it to glory in the past and being forced into a perversion of law and order. In a satiric pamphlet published in 1642, titled *Mad fashions, od fashions, all out of fashions, OR, The Emblems of these distracted times*, John Tay-

20 John William Allen, *English Political Thought*, I, 302–303.

lor captures this recurrent theme in his description of an England metamorphosed. His opening lines, which describe the title-page emblem of a man standing on his head, vividly fuse the various sources of threat:

> The Picture that is Printed in the front
> Is like this Kingdome, if you look upon't:
> For if you well doe note it as it is,
> It is a Transform'd Metamorphasis.
> This Monstrous Picture plainely doth declare
> This land (quite out of order) out of square.
> His Breeches on his shoulders doe appeare,
> His doublet on his lower parts doth weare;
>
> . . . .
>
> The Church o're turnd (a lamentable show)
> The candlestick above, the light below,
> The Cony hunts the Dogge, the Rat the Cat,
> The Horse doth whip the Cart (I pray marke that)
> The Wheelbarrow doth drive the man (oh Base)
> And Eeles and Gudgeons fle a mighty pace.
> And sure this is a Monster of strange fashion,
> That doth surpass all *Ovids* Transformation.
> And this is Englands case this very day,
> All things are turn'd the Cleane contrary way. . . .[21]

When confronted with a troubled time which seemed quite mad, Taylor, like many men then and now, longed for the past. For men of the 1640's England's past was the age of Elizabeth, a time which appeared more ordered, sane, and fruitful than their own; a time somehow more natural:

> For England hath no likelyhood, or show
> Of what it was but seventy yeeres agoe;
> Religion, manners, life and shapes of men,
> Are much unlike the people that were then,
> Nay Englands face and language is estrang'd,
> That all is Metamorphis'd, chop'd and chang'd,
> For like as on the Poles, the VVorld is whorl'd
> So is this Land the *Bedlam* of the VVorld.[22]

[21] *The Works of John Taylor,* Publications of the Spenser Society, no. 7.
[22] Ibid.

The present was only a gloomy reminder of a happier past and a cause of concern for the future.

The Allegory and Pastoral

A moral allegory with political overtones, *Time's Distractions* reflects a pacifist, conservative, Royalist view of England's crisis, a view which is very like Taylor's. It is difficult and somewhat misleading to separate the play's political themes from its moral ones, for the play so pervasively implies a conservative political ethic that its politics are its morality. Just as the distraction of Time separates Judgment from Virtue and hides Honor from the world's eye, so the play insists that without a foundation of rule and authority to produce a healthy social and political climate, morality itself ceases as all becomes "perverted and abused to ruin" (ll. 112–113).

Like many allegorists, the playwright does not treat the allegorical significance of his characters and events rigidly. Uninterested in depicting specific events and actual political figures, he concentrates on showing in general terms the causes and effects of England's social and political convulsions, creating a general rather than a precise relationship between the characters and events of the play and those of English history.

The play early establishes a contrast between two different societies, Arcadia and "the world," which embody two visions of the one political structure of England, visions which bear the relationship of dream to nightmare, of wish fulfillment to madness, and of a myth of bygone glory to a reality of present shame. In the first acts of the play, Arcadia is an emblematic version of an idealized pastoral society in which Will, Judgment, Virtue, Love, and even Fortune can function as they were originally intended to do, free from the perversions of men. Shepherds tend sheep, fishermen fish, servants serve; all are contented in their proper roles. Such is the paradise "to which the only happy of the world / Have wisely from the world retired themselves" (ll. 54–55).

But a dream cannot permanently protect against reality, and

13

the world imposes itself upon Arcadia, an imposition heralded first by the arrival of Danger and then by the appearance of Time. Time's reliance upon Security opens Arcadia to infection from the world, to the venom of Envy and her brood—to the moral and political evils which simultaneously threaten to turn the world to chaos. Because sedition arises from envy, envy is a political problem. As Francis Bacon says in his essay "On Envy" (1625), "It is a disease, in a State, like to Infection. For as Infection, spreadeth upon that, which is sound, and tainteth it; So when *Envy*, is gotten once into a State, it traduceth even the best Actions thereof, and turneth them into an ill Odour. . . ."[23] By means of Envy's infection of Time in Arcadia, the world subsumes the Arcadian dream, and Arcadia becomes an emblem of the reality for which it had originally provided an escape. Only the power and authority of Juno, the Arcadian queen and heavenly goddess, make possible the purgation and expulsion of the sources of Arcadia's infection and thus the restoration of concord upon which the Arcadian dream depends.

By emphasizing the contrast between Arcadia and the world in the first three acts and by bringing the two together in the fourth and the beginning of the fifth acts, the playwright constantly reiterates his apprehension of a distorted society. The world which, in theatrical terms, is initially distanced by its purely verbal existence is foregrounded by the action when Arcadia is itself infected in acts 3 and 4. The description of the world in acts 1 and 2 anticipates the appearance in Arcadia of Danger, Time, Envy, and, finally, of distracted Time in acts 2 and 3, until the condition of Arcadia becomes so thoroughly diseased that by act 4 none but Juno escapes its effects. "Where the Time overflows with venom," says Time at the close of act 3, "that overwhelms the clime" (ll. 576–577).

Although its inhabitants are ostensibly nymphs and swains, it is clear that this Arcadia differs from those of Elizabethan pastoral or of the courtly pastoral plays which delighted King Charles

[23] Quoted from Helen C. White, Ruth C. Wallerstein, and Ricardo Quintana (eds.), *Seventeenth Century Verse and Prose*, p. 53.

14

and Queen Henrietta Maria. Following the vogue set by Walter Montague's *Shepherd's Paradise*,[24] most pastoral plays of the 1630's and early 1640's are highly artificial, sentimental romances, the common plot of which is the creation and unraveling of thwarted love affairs between beautiful, virtuous ladies and their valiant, handsome suitors. The only resemblances between these pastorals and *Time's Distractions* are their common setting in a land temporally and spatially remote and their common rejection of a mimetic representation of the real world. The courtly pastoral removes itself from the world in order to escape it; *Time's Distractions* removes itself as an artistic device in order to understand that world and to re-create it.

Conventions of the earlier, Elizabethan pastoral do, however, appear in the play, but the twist which the playwright gives them emphasizes his political intention. Normally, pastoral embodies a contrast, implied or expressed, between the shepherd's life and some more complex type of civilization; the country in its contented simplicity opposes the court in its anxious complexity. Thus, the idea of a "golden age," a "fiction of an age of simplicity and innocence,"[25] is an inherent part of pastoral; the pastoral aim is to return nostalgically to its innocent, simple beginnings in antiquity.

The first act of the play emphasizes a similar impulse to return to innocence and concord. The initial, conventional description of Arcadia recalls the Golden Age: the first appearance of Fortune and Virtue, who in "amity together" discuss the original similarity of their gifts before man's perversion of them, contrasts the health and concord of Arcadia with the disease and disorder of the world. Age, too, professes the pastoral ideal when he describes his earlier contemplative life, serving Virtue in an idyllic state of nature:

> I lived in solitary hermitage.
> By wholesome labor for my daily food,

---

[24] Acted at court on January 9, 1633.
[25] After Walter W. Greg, *Pastoral Poetry and Pastoral Drama*, pp. 4ff.

15

> To maintain life unto no other end
> But that my hands might not be void of work,
> Nor my heart empty of devotion.
>
> [822–826]

The nostalgia in the play is not, however, primarily for the mythic Golden Age. One may concede the moral superiority of a life of days spent "in contemplation of Virtue" (1. 431), but one's impulses are as well for golden days of a very different sort. The nostalgia in Love's speech in act 3, one of the finest in the play, is not felt for a lost state of innocence but for a "merry" time when "gloves, / Scarfs, garters, chains, and ribbons passed / Fearless and freely and were worn for favors" (ll. 533–535), a courtly time of "golden days" ended not by the corrupting influences of civilization, but by an Honor that is "stern, strict, full of doubts, denials, taunts, repulses" (ll. 542–543). A courtly society by itself is not always so praised in the play, but nowhere is it suggested as the source of the disease in Arcadia or the world.

Although *Time's Distractions* gives token acknowledgment to the ethical stance of pastoral by supporting a contemplative life of innocence and in the nature of its praise of Juno recalls the connection between Elizabethan pastoral and the glorification of the queen, its intention is not that of pastoral. The play neither develops nor reflects a tension between a life of pastoral simplicity and one of courtly complexity. In fact, because the movement of the action is towards the court, towards the construction of a new society based on the reign of Juno, the direction of the ethical ideal in *Time's Distractions* is the exact reverse of that in pastoral. When, after Fortune's arrival in Arcadia, Sight happily predicts, "our very sheep shall dance more courtly than the damoisel of France" (1. 172), he amusingly suggests this reversal although the comment is ironic. If courtiers can become shepherds, sheep might learn to behave like courtiers. The jest has a point. As the play progresses and the Arcadian society is disrupted, the characters learn that peace and concord cannot be assumed but must be constructed by the conscious acquiescence of men to order and authority. The pastoral condition of harmonious innocence

16

dissolves when confronted with Danger and Time, and from that point Arcadia moves away from a pastoral society and toward a type of monarchy.

In its initial freedom from disease Arcadia is contrasted with the world, with reality, but in its clear differentiation of social levels—from the crown to servants—Arcadia suggests a model for that world and another departure from conventional pastoral. An emblem of prelapsarian society, Arcadia usually implies harmony and concord; a queen, when present, exists there only to be lauded and to increase the joy of the inhabitants, not to create and maintain order by the power of her authority. In *Time's Distractions*, on the other hand, Juno behaves very like an ideal monarch. She presides over a court which, like any court, enjoys singing, dancing, and witty banter. As she commands and reprimands her subjects, hears suits, makes matches, and purges her land of the evils that threaten it, her rule is just, wise, and absolute. Even Time finally submits to her and concedes, "To obey you I must" (l. 829).

Because the one pastoral convention which the play consistently maintains is its glorification of the queen-deity figure of Juno, she inevitably recalls Elizabeth, Spenser's Gloriana:

> Great and most glorious virgin Queene alive,
> That with her soveraine powre, and scepter shene,
> All Faery Lond does peacably sustene.
> In widest ocean she her throne does reare,
> That over all the earth it may be seene;
> As morning sunne her beams dispredden cleare,
> And in her face faire peace and mercy doth
>   appeare.
>   [*FQ*, 2.2.11]

William Empson believes that "it was this Renaissance half-worship of Elizabeth and the success of England under her rule that gave conviction to the whole set of ideas" which are pastoral,[26] and it may be that the play's departure from those ideas suggests the playwright's recognition that if the pastoral ideal once accu-

---

26 William Empson, *Some Versions of Pastoral*, p. 34.

rately reflected the concord and harmony of England, then "those golden days are gone" (l. 542) and "this Time has undone us all" (l. 803).

Certainly the play's emphasis on Age and Time makes nostalgia an important theme. The playwright's world is not so harmonious that it can be imitated unself-consciously in a mythic Golden Age or criticized by pastoral standards so divorced from the reality of impending political and social chaos. The significance of the events of the 1640's to every facet of life disallowed the alternative of a contemplative life and a return to innocence in a green Arcadian world. If they are not to become trivialized by absurd artificiality, like milking cows at Trianon, pastoral values are viable only in a time of relative political stability and social harmony, and a contemplative ethic is morally sound only in a time which does not require action. In creating an idyllic Arcadia and destroying it by the distractions of the times, the playwright indicates his recognition of the conflict between the pastoral mode and the play's political intention. In making the restoration of Arcadia's concord dependent upon the power and authority of a mythic queen, he returns his audience to an emblem of monarchy and an England of a merrier time. In emphasizing the value of loving submission to authority and the necessity of recognizing and guarding against Danger and Envy, he offers it direction and a hope for the present. The political aims of *Time's Distractions* are thus closely tied to the playwright's manipulation of pastoral convention, and the ways in which he fulfills and denies the expectations created by an Arcadian setting suggest a conscious and imaginative choice, a scheme for his play which one can only wish were more deftly realized.

Critique

The various classifications of *Time's Distractions* as a "masque," a "political allegory," a "pastoral," and a "morality" suggest either that these genres have certain inherent similarities or that the play is sheer chaos, which it is not. Like the plays in those genres with which it has been associated—genres which move away from mimesis toward ritual and tend to deny the normal dramatic drive—in *Time's Distractions* neither the narrative structure nor the psychological realism of its characters is important. The play develops instead by means of a contrast of opposites—of life-giving and death-dealing forces—revealed in character, imagery, and structure.

The action of *Time's Distractions* is what Northrop Frye describes as "ternary," an action which ritually is "like a contest of summer and winter in which winter occupies the middle action."[27] The intention of the first section of the play is to show the paradisiacal nature of Arcadia and the process of its formation into a society. The middle section, the longest, focuses on the infection of Arcadia and the results of that infection on its inhabitants. The final section restores Arcadia and re-creates it as an ordered society. In its moral and political implications, the action describes time past, time present, and time future.

The play's point of view is time present, and from that point of view the action raises three questions which it attempts to answer: Who or what is to blame for the metamorphosis of Time? What are the effects of Time's "apostasy" on society? What is required to restore this mad society to sanity? The action moves by means of a series of scenes, grouping different characters who reveal facets of the Arcadian world in its several stages. Acts 1 and 2 describe the nature of Arcadia and by means of the arrivals of Juno, Fortune and Virtue, and Love establish criteria for a society still in formation. The climactic moments of this section occur in the harmony of the dances, the first with Juno, Fortune, and Virtue and the second when swains and nymphs surround Love, "crowning his deity our king" (1. 287). Arcadian harmony is shattered immediately after the second dance when Danger arrives. Act 3 opens with the first appearance of Time. Relying upon Security, who denies Danger's presence in Arcadia, Time falls asleep and is infected by Envy and her brood—Suspicion, Spite, Malice, Jealousy, Fear, Necessity—all evils which separate

[27] Northrop Frye, *The Anatomy of Criticism*, p. 171.

19

men from one another and make a cohesive society impossible. The now-distracted Time meets Age and Love. No longer appearing in his true image, the disguised Love is a servant of Age. Time immediately infects Age, who recovers, momentarily, at the sight of Juno, Fortune, Virtue, and Honor. They join in a dance which temporarily restores harmony until Time, too, joins it and mars their sport by infecting everyone but Juno and scattering the dancers. Arcadia is now thoroughly infected and divided. By means of a series of six processionlike scenes observed by Juno "above" and Time "below," act 4 depicts the effects of Time's distractions on all levels of Arcadian society. In the final scene of the act, Juno takes control, promising to purge Time, and calls upon her satyrs to expel Danger. The final act restores Arcadia. With the help of Age and Love, Juno purges Time and then arranges matches between Age and Honor, Will and Desert, Judgment and Virtue, and Fortune and Love, creating "strong bonds" on which to base the Arcadian society of the future.

By choosing an Arcadian setting for his action and by populating it with mythological and moral figures, the playwright has created the usual problem in characterization for allegorical drama: his characters must be sufficiently compatible with the iconography of their names to be recognized and accepted by an audience, yet they must depart enough from convention to create dramatic interest. The principal technique which he uses to solve this problem is to capitalize on the ambiguities and connotations inherent in the characters' names. Character is thus defined in action, and the meaning of a character changes in the context of different scenes so that he can serve at one point a moral purpose and at another a political and, occasionally, a pastoral one. Sometimes this technique succeeds in creating variety and interest, but more often it falters and confuses the focus. An analysis of the way in which the characters are manipulated suggests the play's strengths and weaknesses as well as the playwright's methods for making his basic metaphors concrete.

As a microcosm of the world, the Arcadian society is made up of various social and symbolic levels. At the top are three author-

20

ity figures: Juno, Time, and Age, each of whom has a controlling influence on the rest of Arcadia in the power inherent in their names. Immediately below them are six virtues—Virtue, Fortune, Honor, Desert, Will, and Judgment. Socially and morally, they are the ruling class whose dissension creates chaos and whose bonds provide a foundation for an ordered society. Love is of their class but has a greater symbolic significance. The lower classes are represented by Sight and Search, who are the servants of Will and Judgment; Simplicity, the fisherman; and the groups of Arcadian nymphs and swains. Eventually expelled, the evil characters, Danger and Envy and her brood, do not figure in Arcadia's class structure, but serve as the forces for dissension. Security, morally neutral, is the mistress of Time, but she is excluded from the new society at the play's conclusion.

As an earthly and heavenly queen, Juno serves a monarchal and quasi-religious function. Her power, suspended during the period of Arcadia's infection,[28] emerges when Danger is expelled and Time purged, and she becomes the true ruler and re-creator of her kingdom. In act 1, by assuming the role of Lucina, the goddess of parturition (l. 125),[29] Juno explicitly promises to protect Arcadia against sterility and links herself to fruition: as midwife Lucina, she will lead Honor forth from darkness into light. Juno is by no means omnipotent against the forces of destruction, however. Although Time and Age both finally submit to her, they manage to control and metamorphize Arcadia for a while. Juno's function is consistent, and her power is acknowledged from her first appearance, but it is not until the third stage of the action, when Arcadia has been instructed by Time's scourge and Age and

---

[28] The play implies at one time that she can take control whenever she wishes (ll. 582–587), but the action suggests rather that Age, Time, and Love have temporarily overthrown her rule. This is one of the points which the action needs to define more sharply.

[29] In assuming this role Juno suggests that she takes on the powers of Venus and Diana, both of whom often served as Lucina. Etymologically, the word is associated with the moon ("little light") and, therefore, also with madness. Juno does serve as Lucina to the entire Arcadian society when she brings it out of madness in act 5.

Time acknowledge her as their "sovereign deity," that she becomes the queen of an ordered, harmonious community.

Time enters only after the appearance of Danger in Arcadia has signaled the extremity to which the natural and psychological balance has been upset in the present. Time is principally a visual metaphor for the present—the times—but he also is temporality and, occasionally, the past. His actions, true to popular iconography, also "scourge" Arcadia and ultimately reveal the play's truth: that order is predicated on loving submission to authority.[30]

When he first appears, Age is a prototype of virtuous old age, living a contemplative life and serving Virtue, and as such he suggests the values of a pastoral life and of the past. When Time infects him (or before),[31] he falls prey to wanton love and becomes a lecherous old man, a type anticipating those of Restoration comedy. He is also the age: by forgetting duty to his "sovereign goddess" (l. 811), in his prideful self-love[32] he creates the conditions which make possible Time's infection. After he recognizes his error and submits to Juno's rule, Age can assist her to purge Time.

Because they both stand for the present, Time and Age are similar and mutually dependent. The allegory suggests that when a given period of time, an age, becomes rash, willful, and wanton and turns away from loving concord and submission to authority, it makes possible the entrance of Danger. If, then, at the moment of danger the time is overreliant on its sense of security and so

[30] See Erwin Panofsky, *Studies in Iconology*, pp. 69–93. A number of the images associated with Time in the play also appear in Time's speech as Chorus in *The Winter's Tale*, 4.1.

[31] Here again is some confusion. In the play's action, Age is clearly changed by Time, but when he blames Time for his infection in act 5, Juno reprimands him, saying that Age created the conditions for Time's infection by Envy. Age then recalls that he "took in" wanton love and admits his share of the responsibility.

[32] Signified by his desire for a mirror and concern with his appearance (ll. 456–465), a common medieval and Renaissance emblem. His trouble with his sight in the same scene suggests, iconographically, moral defectiveness.

22

becomes slothful,[33] the times and the age become perverted and chaotic, and everything turns upside down. Before a return to order is possible, the age must submit to rule and the times must be purged of the forces of disorder.

The alternatives for society of chaos and order are symbolized in the play by Danger and Love. What is represented by Danger, initially ambiguous, is clarified in each of his several appearances. Danger first enters Arcadia immediately following the dance in which the natural Arcadians, the nymphs and swains, had crowned Love their deity. He scatters the group and destroys the harmony which that dance suggested. In later appearances, Danger continues to thwart love. He prevents the marriage of Will and Desert, and he prevents Desert from returning Love's bow and arrows, weapons lost originally when Love was in the service of Will.[34] Without his weapons to signify his godliness, Love is powerless against Danger; after Danger's first appearance, Love remains disguised until the purgation of Time. The appearance of Danger also precedes the first entry of Time, and Danger's expulsion, significantly by satyrs, creates the proper conditions for Time's purgation. Danger, it becomes clear, is that which blocks Love and creates dissension. It is linked to the powers of destruction, war, disease, and sterility and so interrupts the re-creative powers of man and nature which challenge Time.

The symbolic opposition between Love and Danger is reinforced in a consistent, recurrent pattern of images related to an antithesis of sterility and fertility. The fecund deliveries in Arcadia of Honor and of Cupid[35] are set against the fecal produc-

[33] Because he falls asleep; sleeping commonly signified sloth in medieval and Renaissance iconography.

[34] This point is almost lost in the play, but I think it is significant to both levels of the allegory. See lines 210, 215.

[35] The discussion of Honor's birth and growth receives a good bit of attention. One reason Envy gives for her infection of Time is to prevent Honor from marrying, hence proliferating (ll. 372–378), and Virtue suggests that she can "stop her growth and blast her glories" (l. 654). I see the manner of Cupid's entrance as a birth, or rebirth, primarily because he makes an explicit comparison with the birth of Venus, but also because the efforts to pull him up parody labor (ll. 185–206).

23

tions of Time, who "full of stuff" is purged of Envy and her brood, libels, swearing oaths, and lies; he is purged of that which divides and destroys. The imagery contrasts peace with war, "entire" friendship with enmity, health with disease, sanity with madness. It is clear that the major threat to the distracted Arcadian world is barrenness, the sterility which marks an age that has inverted the right order of rule, has become torn by dissension, and has made love and authority powerless.

Frequently represented as the first major deity to arise from chaos, Love assumes, in part, the function of Venus, particularly as she represents the great generative force in nature and the only power capable of neutralizing the destructive principle symbolized mythologically by Mars and here by Danger. The idea that Love alone can temper strife and hatred is a Renaissance commonplace. In myth, however, there are both two Venuses and two Cupids, and their roles are antithetical. Improperly directed, love turns inward and becomes self-love, pride, and lechery and is, therefore, destructive. When Age takes in "wanton love" (ll. 819–820), he has turned from creative love to lecherous love. Although Love acts most like the "pretty, witty wag" which he is called—like a playful, sportive Cupid—his symbolic value as generative love or destructive love informs specific scenes.[36]

Less complex in their conception are the play's four female virtues—Fortune, Virtue, Honor, and Desert—and the two male virtues—Judgment and Will. In the first act Fortune and Virtue both require Juno's aid for their preservation and protection from the greedy world. In Arcadia, Fortune divests herself of her usual attributes: her wings, which indicate fickleness, and the turning wheel by which she raises men and nations to great heights only to cast them down again. Instead, under Juno's rule she returns to her original purpose: to deliver Honor.

[36] One love is the traditional Venus, daughter of Uranus and born from the sea. Love associates himself with her at his entrance (see note 35). The other is the daughter of Zeus-Jupiter and Dione-Juno. Love refers to Juno as his "aunt" (ll. 507, 803, 806), which implies that the writer was conscious of the two conceptions. See Panofsky, *Iconology*, pp. 142–143.

24

Except when they are used to serve the political allegory, the other virtues are what their names signify. Desert, appropriately, is a rather static character, acted upon rather than acting. True to traditional moral philosophy, Judgment's supremacy over Will is stressed; Judgment prevents Will from behaving rashly and keeps him from going astray. Judgment marries Virtue, supports order, and is consistently Will's moral superior. In the fourth act the inverted relationship between Judgment and Will suggests the power struggle between Crown and Parliament, as Honor occasionally represents Puritan morality, "stern, strict, full of doubts, denials" (ll. 542–543). The political implications of the characters' relationships are usually quite clear from the context.[37]

Sight and Search, who are not very distinguishable, open the play, and during their necessary—and plodding—exposition they are the pastoral shepherds of tradition. Some attempt is made to endow them with a moral significance (they are the servants of Will and Judgment), but that meaning becomes almost totally subordinated to their role as types of the lower classes. Although they at times have the wit and charm of the *zanni* in *commedia dell'arte*, they have their moral ambiguity as well, and the play's point of view primarily finds them greedy, socially ambitious, rash, and somewhat stupid. At the close of act 1 Juno has promised to protect Fortune from the "greedy world" which would have ripped open her womb; at the beginning of act 2 Sight and Search are greedily reveling in the thought that a share of all the world will soon be theirs. The birth of Honor means for them "towns, towers, castles" (l. 150), and opportunity to rise to great heights socially and politically. Sight tells Judgment that "this year is enough to make every knave in the cards a king," for "we are all made masters" (ll. 169–170). Judgment reflects the play's point of view towards such pretensions: "You are mad" (l. 171). Sight and Search (and to a lesser extent, Simplicity), though sometimes the shepherds of pastoral convention, figure more of-

[37] As Honor's is. Nevertheless, it is somewhat disconcerting to have Honor function both as a highly desired ideal and as a repressive force. The two levels of Will and Judgment, on the other hand, work very well.

25

ten in the political allegory as rabble which must be firmly controlled by authority.

The other characters are straightforward emblems; their names are their *significatio*. Envy and her brood represent the various moral causes of political and social dissension, and Security personifies the frequent Renaissance meaning of her name: presumptuous lack of caution, carelessness. The swains, nymphs, and satyrs serve the play's gesture towards its pastoral setting, as does Will in his occasional role of pastoral lover. Mythological symbols of the luxuriant forces of Nature, the satyrs are as well an appropriate choice to trample down and expel Danger.

Although the political allegory is implicit in the relationship between some of the characters and in the behavior or dialogue of others throughout the play, it controls the meaning only in act 4. Past error has produced the present upheaval, and Arcadia in its distractions here merges with the world. Even though the relationship between the characters and contemporary events remains loose, it is safe to make a fairly close connection between this act and the playwright's perception of the troubles of his time.

Structured like a procession with one group of characters replacing another, the act includes seven brief scenes in which the Arcadians show the thoroughness of Time's infection throughout all levels of society. Progressing linearly, the act begins with Time in control and ends with the expulsion of Danger and Juno's authority uppermost. Played with "Juno above" and "Time below" as observers of the action, the act is a symbolic struggle between them to determine Arcadia's future. The first scene depicts the most significant effect of the "apostasy" of Time. The right order of rule between Judgment and Will has been inverted: Judgment (the Crown) has been "thrust out of office" (l. 593) and no longer controls Will (Parliament), who refuses to acknowledge Judgment's supremacy. "Thou thine own neck shall break," Judgment predicts to the "rash, giddy fool" as they exit, quarreling (ll. 590–595).

26

The next scene between Sight and Search shows the effects on the masses of this upset in authority. They hurl scatological invective, accuse one another of spying "for some weak statesman" or for sergeants (ll. 605–607). Joined by Simplicity, they fight "for example and for fashion's sake" only because "all the shepherds in Arcadia are at it and they know not what for" (ll. 637–638). In these scenes the trio is quite explicitly associated with the London apprentices whose rioting and petitioning in support of Parliament helped to deliver the city into its hands and to strengthen Parliament's own war faction.

With both the authority of the state and its lower classes in disarray, it is natural that Fortune and Virtue should resume their former contention. Their scene makes primarily a metaphoric point: when the times are in chaos, neither Fortune nor Virtue ensures survival. The "blood and horror in the fields of war" (l. 669) are, Fortune claims, the works of Virtue as often as they are of Fortune, and when the time creates a need for her, Fortune turns her back on men (ll. 680–682).

Two more virtues rip one another apart in the following scene between Love and Honor. In their quarrel, each presents a false alternative to the other, and each denies a value important to human life: Honor (in her Puritan role) would have no mirth, pleasure, sport, or free pastimes (l. 703); Love would have nothing else and would deny as well any value to reputation, honor, fame, and glory (ll. 706–707). Together their values create one whole; separated, Honor destroys and Love ruins. No compromise is possible with two such rigidly opposed positions, and their argument finally ends only by force. Honor becomes a prisoner of Time, who hides her in his dungeon to obscure her from the world's eye. The quarrel between Love and Honor illustrates the way in which positions become rigidified and values distorted in a period of political turmoil. By implication, it also calls attention to the need for compromise on both sides. Without it, argument ends in force, and once force is used, Honor is hidden.

The progression leads to Age. He appears alone, complaining

of his lack of success with the nymphs. "Here," the playwright seems to say, "this is the Age. In the midst of chaos, it is vain, lecherous, and foolish. In a society torn apart, Age sings of bouncing buttocks." Desert and Danger soon enter, and Age, seeing Desert only as a nymph "weary of her maidenhead" (l. 756), recklessly ignores Danger to pursue her. Danger raises his club to kill Age, and only a last-minute rescue saves him. Politically, this final scene in the procession of Arcadia's perversion has led to a disastrous precipice for Age. Concerned only with his vain and foolish lechery, Age ignores genuine Danger. Age and Security enable Time to capture Desert, and now all the virtues are hidden and starving in Time's dungeon.

The play envisions a society which has turned aside from those values which make life harmonious and creative for each man and from the order and degree which give a country continuity and stability. The image of metamorphosis pervades the play. Time in his madness asks, "Who or what am I?" (l. 396) and believes himself bewitched (l. 433); Age wonders, "Was not I Age but now?" (ll. 448–449); Love's true identity is hidden behind a disguise of wantonness and servility; Sight grows "purblind"; Search, palsied; Will, lame; and Judgment himself, idiotic. The blame falls on all. Although Age, Time, and Love are variously responsible for Arcadia's disorder, their faults are similar. All neglect duty; all, metaphorically, put themselves before community. In the service of Will, Love loses the arms which made him a god and hence loses his proper power; Age, influenced by wanton love, abandons the contemplation of Virtue and the service of his "sovereign goddess" and thus permits Danger to enter Arcadia; Time falls asleep indulging himself in the sweet music of Security "in spite of Danger" and enables the entire company of vices which divide a society to enter freely. Early in the play Virtue says,

> The world
> Is out of frame; disorder governs it,
> Threatening to turn it all again to chaos,
>
> [93–95]

28

and the action has made that chaos visible. For many men at the time of the Civil War the horror which the Renaissance believed inevitable if once "the specialty of rule hath been neglected" has indeed appeared in their land. The point of view in *Time's Distractions* is identical to that of Ulysses in Shakespeare's *Troilus and Cressida:*

> Take but degree away, untune that string,
> And, hark, what discord follows! Each thing meets
> In mere oppugnancy.
>
> [1.3.109–111]

"The unity and married calm of states" must be returned for a "promise of future peace."

Masque and Dance

When A. H. Bullen first drew attention to this play, he called it a masque, as, more recently, have F. S. Boas and J. D. Jump. Although the play has a generic affinity with the masque, it is not a true masque. As a courtly spectacle structured upon scenic effects, music, and dance—a spectacle which moves towards uniting masquer and spectator—the masque proper differs from *Time's Distractions* in several significant ways. The play offers strong internal evidence that it was performed on a bare platform stage and so offered no spectacle of elaborate and rapidly changing scenery.[38] There is no "taking out" to unite actors and audience at the end—the Arcadian world remains self-contained—and it does not suggest a court audience. The masque is, finally, much more bound up in nonverbal elements than is this play.

Although *Time's Distractions* differs from the paradigmatic masque, it also contains many of its characteristics. In both the movement of its action and its thematic concerns, like the masque it leads towards the court as pastoral leads away from it. Its development of the action by groupings of characters instead of by narrative plot and its compelling drive toward a condition of

[38] See below, pp. 35–37.

29

idealistic harmony and order and a concurrent exposing and expulsion of disharmonious elements are points of structure which arise from the masque, especially as it developed during the latter part of the reign of James I and throughout that of Charles I. It was, perhaps, from Jonson's later masques, which embody the contrast of opposites, that the author learned the technique which so pervades his play.

As the masque developed, it tended to fuse with the moral play. Because the main theme of a masque involves mythological gods, personifications of virtues, fairies, and the like, the figures of the anti-masque tend to become demonic and disruptive. Jonson often managed to incorporate the anti-masque elements into the harmonious society of the conclusion, particularly in his later masques, but more often the dramatic characterization splits into an antithesis of virtue and vice. It is this tendency toward the separation of the two which recalls the morality play, as Milton's *Comus* does, in which the spectacle and celebration become subservient to the conflict between the opposing forces represented by Comus and the Lady.[39] Entertainments like Milton's, part morality and part masque, were not uncommon, particularly in private performances after 1630. The interest in moral masques and morality plays, in part created by the popularity of Thomas Nabbes's *Microcosmus* (1635), persisted in private theatricals throughout the Interregnum.[40] The clear-cut moral distinctions in *Time's Distractions* among the good characters and the mingling of abstractions with virtues and mythological characters are thus as usual in the later Caroline drama as in the court masque.

It is in its use of dance to punctuate the moments of harmony or discord that *Time's Distractions* most clearly imitates the masque.[41] Symbols of unity or disruption, the dances serve as a guide to the changing conditions of Arcadia. The first dance in

[39] See Frye, *Anatomy of Criticism*, p. 290.
[40] Harbage, *Cavalier Drama*, pp. 140, 159–160, 195.
[41] The dances do not, however, conform to the usual arrangement of them in the masque. See Andrew J. Sabol, *Songs and Dances for the Stuart Masque*, p. 1.

the play (ll. 137–138) celebrates the arrival of Juno, Fortune, and Virtue in Arcadia, making visual the harmony of Arcadia, which has been emphasized in dialogue, and the unity among Juno, the goddess-queen, Virtue, and Fortune. The dance in the second act again emphasizes harmony, but on a different level of society, that of the Arcadian nymphs and swains. It also serves as an ironic climax to the first section of the action. Recently pulled up from the sea into Arcadia, Love decides he likes the Arcadian air, but he fears to stay because of "that ugly monster" Danger. Will assures him that "all Arcadia" shall guard him and that he shall "be always armed and attended by a band of lovers" (ll. 277–278). To prove it, a group of swains and nymphs enter, and Sight introduces a ring dance around Love:

> . . . let all the Nymphs and Swains
> With dances and with melody
> Surround his person in a ring,
> Crowning his deity our king.
>
> [285–287]

Like a maypole festivity, the dance is an elemental celebration of Love, an occasion so joyous that it prompts Will to ask, "What more addition or increase / Need we to keep us here in peace?" (ll. 290–291). Danger enters. Love recognizes him and flees, and the Arcadian harmony is shattered. Will speaks for the mood of Arcadia which the entrance of Danger has so totally changed: "Was ever happy peace so soon perverted?" (l. 307).

In the third act the two dances repeat the central event of the act, the infection of Arcadia. At the beginning of the act, Envy, Suspicion, Necessity, Jealousy, Fear, Spite, Mischief, Rancor, and Malice come upon Time and in a parody of the ring dance around Love surround him in their antic dance: Suspicion lays her hands upon his heart, Envy applies her vipers to his eyes and ears, Necessity nips him, and Envy commands all to "laugh and dance to think how mad he'll be / And all Arcadia as mad as he" (ll. 381–389). Although Time has now been infected, except for Age's temporary attack the rest of Arcadia remains normal. Honor has

31

been born, and she joins Fortune, Virtue, and Juno to "revel" with Love and Age in Age's bower. After a scene of courtly banter, Juno reminds the group that "we do not what we came for / To grace old Age's bower with measure" (ll. 555–556) and tells Age, "be lively now and jump with us" (l. 560). The six dance, but "in the midst of the dance, Time enters" (ll. 561–562). As the entrance of Danger signaled the disorder of a previously harmonious society, so now all try to run away from Time as he begins to spread his infection. Except Juno, they cannot do so, and Arcadia is overwhelmed with the venom of Time.

The visual symbol for the distractions of Arcadia in the fourth act is the dance of Sight, Search, and Simplicity. Quarreling for no reason, they sing of the madness to which their action attests, concluding, "We all must be mad; 'tis the price of our pain. / All mortals are mad when the mad planets reign" (ll. 631–632). Finally, they decide that since all the other shepherds are doing it, they had best fight too, so they "dance, kick, and beat each other" before they exit "halting off" (ll. 645–646). By the end of the act, Juno has resumed control and promises to relieve Arcadia and to purge Time. As the entrance of Danger marked the end of the first mood of Arcadian harmony, so his expulsion marks its return. Taking advantage of his being disarmed, Juno calls forth her satyrs, commanding them to "triumph over Danger in your dances" (l. 793). During the dance, the satyrs "trample and abuse him. Danger roars" (ll. 793–794). This done, Juno can now "restore to my Arcadia / The peace and happiness which she had before" (ll. 796–797), the "happy peace perverted" in act 2 when Danger first entered.

The play concludes with a dance which symbolizes the foundation of a new order of society. Time purged, Arcadia restored, and couples matched, "all the whole kingdom here of Love" is now happy (l. 994). The evil within them expelled, all orders of Arcadian society are for the first time on stage together for the concluding cosmic dance. Juno tells her subjects, "Each take his own by the hand and let us move / To tread out mischief and replant true love" (ll. 1002–1003). The couples dance, and Arcadia shouts for joy because, as Juno tells the audience, "Those are strong bonds after a sad decrease / For a confirmation of a future peace" (ll. 1007–1008).

The pattern made by all the dances, which reinforce the thematic concerns and the basic symbols of the play, suggests that the playwright intentionally used masque elements for much the same reason that he drew upon pastoral convention—to celebrate monarchy and the ordered society which depends upon the Crown. By means of the magic of words, dance, spectacle, and song, the masque celebrated the ideal which the audience believed it possessed; this play celebrates instead those ideals to which its author hopes society will return through order and love.

Performance

The date of the play and its political implications make the question of performance a particularly intriguing one. Although the play has been categorized as probable closet drama,[42] Time's Distractions has few of the long speeches and pages of dialogue unbroken by action which typify the static closet drama. Rather, the rapid succession of scenes, the implied and specifically directed action, the dances, and the processions keep the stage in constant flux. In its clearly stated or implicit production requirements and in its attention to the details of stage business, the play consistently attests that its author expected performance.

The final two scenes in act 4 are not the most effective in the play either dramatically or theatrically, but they are typical of the way in which the play appeals to an audience's fondness for rapidly paced action and variety in incident and character. In only seventy-five lines of dialogue the audience is entertained with two songs—one delightfully bawdy—the complaint of Age to the audience of his lack of success in tripping up a nymph, a threatened death and a last-minute rescue, the abduction of a maiden, and a dance in which a group of satyrs very satisfactorily

[42] Harbage and Schoenbaum, Annals of English Drama, p. 145.

trample and abuse Danger while he, understandably, roars. During this time the stage has demanded constant attention. Four different characters and six dancers enter and leave, and even during the few moments when the action slackens, the audience's eye continues to move, its attention directed by a line from Juno, who sits above the stage, or one from Time, seated below, probably at front left or right, then back again to center stage for the main action. In such ways the play consistently demonstrates a recognition of what constitutes audience appeal and the ability to deal, more or less smoothly, with theatrical necessities like the problem of getting the sleeping Age off the stage at the end of act 4. The frequent dances and songs and the processions in act 5 of Time's purged vices and of metamorphosed Arcadians—a procession of misfits in which "they all show action accordingly"—all would be purely gratuitous and rather nonsensical if the play had not been intended for performance.

As the above discussion of masque and dance has suggested, many of the most significant moments of the play are, in fact, primarily theatrical. When Time is purged, the imaginative appeal of hearing Time's offstage sufferings combines with the visual interest of seeing his purged vices scamper across the stage, cowing and ducking from Love's hearty kicks. The scene creates an impression of evil that suggests its nature as both real and ludicrous, and in performance it would oblige even the dullest member of the audience to recognize the symbolic importance of Love as he physically drives out Envy, Suspicion, Malice, Hatred, and the rest.

The play consistently converts metaphor into action, as when Time hides Honor from the "world's eye" or when Danger is trampled by satyrs. Entrances are carefully timed and scenes juxtaposed to provide dramatic irony: Juno, Fortune, Virtue, and Honor enter just as Age is asking Love to get him a wench; the scene of Time's infection follows the one in which Danger has entered. To heighten the expectations of the audience, a character's first entrance is often anticipated in the dialogue, sometimes several times, as for Danger; or the manner of his entry creates a mystery, as for Love, which serves the same purpose. Care is exhibited with timing as well. In the scene of Danger's first appearance, Will's lack of awareness of his presence gives Danger time to cross the stage and the audience a second or two to wonder who he is, and it sets up the dialogue so that Love, Danger's symbolic antithesis, is the first to recognize him and the first to flee.

To examine such touches as entrances carefully timed to cover a stage crossing or to create dramatic irony may seem to be dwelling on minutiae, and so they are, relatively, for the reader. On stage, however, such attention to theatrical detail can bring a weak play to life; without it, even a strong play falters. The way in which a playwright handles the entrances and exits of characters and the juxtaposition of scenes is often a fair test of his dramatic skill. Usually this author's touch is deft, and he rarely forces dialogue to serve theatrical necessity or to provide essential exposition alone.[43]

In less significant ways, too, the play exhibits its theatrical nature. Occasionally the dialogue depends upon action for complete clarity (for example, ll. 458–459). Asides, sight puns (ll. 318, 582), speeches directed to the audience, and entrances timed for humorous effect theatrically lighten the moralizing.

One can derive some notion of the play's staging and the cast from internal evidence, although the more interesting questions about performance and audience must remain unanswered. The stage required is a simple platform stage without a curtain.[44] The writer was obviously aware of the curtained scenic stage, however, as the allusion in Juno's metaphor to opening a curtain in order to "discover" a scene attests: "That so heaven's curtains being drawn I might / Better discover what is done beneath"

---

[43] When he does, the result is very bad indeed. The expository scene in act 1 between Sight and Search, generally weak, reaches a low point when, to get on with more essential information, Sight says "and so much upon that subject."

[44] Although the stage directions call for all to exit only at the end of one act, it is very clear that they do so consistently. Juno would not have had the satyrs remove Age's sleeping body unless the stage were curtainless.

(ll. 58–59). In fact, the dialogue between Sight and Search which precedes Juno's entrance attempts to create the illusion that she actually does descend surrounded by her Clouds (ll. 43–46), as she did by means of cloud machinery in the masque. Here, however, the Clouds are characters, and all prosaically "enter."

The entire action of the play takes place in one locale, probably innocent of decoration and free to suggest whatever the action of the moment requires. The stage may have been set with a few properties to suggest Arcadia—some trees and a rock, perhaps. Since Fortune "hangs up" her wings, at least one such set piece is likely. Someplace where one or two characters can sit relatively removed from center stage is required, both in act 1, when Sight and Search remain onstage as silent observers for one hundred lines of dialogue, and in act 4, when Time remains seated "below" throughout most of the act. The continued presence onstage of Fortune's wings, removed and hung up in act 1 (ll. 127–128), in act 2 (ll. 180–181, 268), and again in act 5 (l. 997), is strong evidence that there is no change of scene.

As in the Elizabethan theater, changes in locale are provided verbally and not always gracefully: "While thou speaks it of fishing, we are arrived where our masters are a fishing, but let us not mind 'em yet" (ll. 163–164). The awkwardness here and in the earlier expository scene in act 1 is so unlike the author's usual skill in handling theatrical problems that it suggests the possibility that he was more familiar with the scenic stage. On several occasions the dialogue calls for characters to be drawn up or thrust down, implying a stage with a trap and machinery, but the stage directions indicate only an entrance or exit. This disparity between the dialogue and the stage direction could be the result of the play's having been moved to a different type of stage from the one for which it was originally written, a hypothesis which could also account for the manner of Juno's entrance, or the dialogue could simply indicate another attempt to create the illusion of a more elaborate stage than was actually available. In either case, the writer obviously was familiar with stage machinery, and if he felt conscious of a disadvantage in working

36

with a bare stage, he shared that feeling with others of his time.[45]

Throughout most of act 4, Juno is "above," a stage direction which requires a second level, possibly a balcony at the rear of the stage. The musician's balcony, common in the great hall of many manor houses, would serve the need. In any case, nothing is needed for the stage which a modest hall and a few hours of carpentry could not provide. The required hand properties present even fewer difficulties. Fortune's wings might be an exception, but her breakable turning wheel, the net in which Cupid is drawn "up," Desert's (and Love's) bow and quiver, Danger's club, Age's vial, and Will's crutches are common objects.

The play is less explicit about costuming, but what is said suggests a similar simplicity. Costume is mentioned in the stage directions only when the actor has to make a change, as when Age appears wearing "fancies" (ll. 723–724) or when Time enters "bound about the head and hugely in the belly" (l. 827). When the dialogue draws attention to a costume, as it does, twice, to Virtue's and to Love's, it probably does so because the character's costume departs from what is usual for his mythic or allegorical nature.

For a play of this date, the size of the cast might argue against performance, particularly a private, amateur one, if it were not known that a large cast in such productions was fairly common. Mildmay Fane's *Candy Restored*, for example, which was "presented in a shew at Apthorpe the 12th of ffebruary 1640 [that is, 1641] to the Lord and Lady of that place, by some of their owne children and famelie,"[46] requires thirty-six actors, a good-sized

---

[45] Note, for example, the defensiveness in the Prologue to Newcastle's *Country Captain*, acted at Blackfriars about 1640:
Gallants, I'll tell you what we do not mean
To show you here[,] a glorious painted scene,
With various doors to stand instead of wit,
Or richer clothes with lace, for lines well writ;
Tailors and painters thus, your dear delights
May prove your poets only for your sight,
Not understanding. . . .
[46] Mildmay Fane, *Mildmay Fane's "Raguillo D'Oceano," 1640*, IV, 30.

37

family. The cast necessary to perform *Time's Distractions* is smaller, but even taking doubling practices into account, the play requires a minimum of twenty-two actors and dancers, with nine male and five female speaking parts and eight walk-ons and dancers plus, probably, several musicians. No doubt the dancing roles were doubled; the swains who dance in act 2 are probably the satyrs of act 4, and Juno's Clouds in act 1 are the nymphs of act 2 and Envy's brood in acts 3 and 4. Security, who, interestingly, is the only speaking character not listed in the "Nomina Actorum," could be doubled by Honor, since the two characters do not appear on stage together and their separate appearances allow sufficient time for a costume change. The actors required to be on stage for the final scene make any further doubling impossible.

Without an extant cast list, one cannot determine whether the original cast, if any, was professional or amateur, but amateurs were considered by many to rival the excellence of professionals.[47] The assignment of the songs in the play raises the possibility that the playwright wrote with specific actors in mind, at least for some of the parts. Age and Security sing most of the songs, Age having three and Security two, which indicates the availability of two actors with good voices.

Where the play was performed, if in fact it was, is an equal mystery. I have no doubt that it was intended for production, but beyond that, one can only conjecture. Throughout the war and the Interregnum the county seats of the nobility perpetuated the vogue for amateur theatricals begun in the 1630's and increasingly common in the 1640's. We now know that there was considerably more dramatic activity between 1642 and 1660 than formerly was presumed. Even the public theaters continued playing sporadically in the early years of the war; Professor Hotson cites evidence for public performances in August, September, and October, 1643, for example.[48] Plays and players (almost without exception Royalists) followed the court to Holland, Oxford, and

[47] Harbage, *Cavalier Drama*, p. 193.
[48] Hotson, *Commonwealth and Restoration Stage*, p. 17.

Paris. In 1642 and 1643 the plays to entertain the court at Oxford were sometimes performed by amateurs and sometimes by the Blackfriars actors, the King's Men, who were then serving as soldiers in the Royal Army.[49] Although private performance seems the most likely of the various possibilities, the play is decidedly not courtly even with its upper-class and Royalist bias. *Time's Distractions* certainly would have been an unlikely choice to cheer the king and queen at Oxford. Who did hear it and how they received it, if, indeed, it found an audience, one can only guess.

Sources and Analogues

With the exception of George Chapman's *Byron's Tragedy*, it is very difficult to determine with any assurance of accuracy the sources for this play.[50] Its characters, imagery, and thematic concerns are all derived from the seventeenth-century storehouse of emblem literature, moral philosophy, and classical mythology which virtually every poet and playwright drew upon. Many of the phrases and images in the play have a familiar ring for that reason, and usually they can be traced to a number of different sources. Debts which the playwright appears to owe to Jonson's masques, for example, can also be traced to Spenser, and whether the playwright drew from Jonson or Spenser or another source is frequently impossible to determine, partially because his characteristic method is to imitate or to paraphrase, not to duplicate.

The resemblances between *Time's Distractions* and the masque scene in Chapman's *Byron's Tragedy*, to which Bullen first called attention, does, however, mark Chapman as a direct source.[51] Chapman's "masque" is, in actuality, an exceedingly long speech

[49] Harbage, *Cavalier Drama*, p. 207; Hotson, *Commonwealth and Restoration Stage*, pp. 8, 9.

[50] The masque scene from *Byron's Tragedy* is appended, and a number of analogues are given in the explanatory notes. All quotations from Chapman are from *The Plays of George Chapman*, ed. Thomas Marc Parrott.

[51] Bullen, *Old English Plays*, II, 428–429.

made by Cupid as presenter and broken into two parts by music and a dance. Both parts are court compliments: the first "figures" the reconciliation of the king's mistress and queen, and the second is a riddle, the answer to which is "good fame." The author of *Time's Distractions* may originally have been drawn to *Byron's Tragedy* because it concerns sedition, and he found in the masque an allegory which could serve his own purpose. Having primarily an allegorical function in his own play, Chapman's masque is static, and the anonymous playwright's technique is to convert Cupid's speech into dramatic action and concrete characters.

The second half of the "masque," the riddle, is of little importance to *Time's Distractions*, although some of Honor's speeches may have been suggested by it. Although the author does not directly imitate them, the first nineteen lines of the masque influenced several of his scenes and relationships between characters. Cupid presents to the king

> . . . these nymphs, part of the scatter'd train
> Of friendless Virtue (living in the woods
> Of shady Arden, and of late not hearing
> The dreadful sounds of war, but that sweet Peace,
> Was by your valour lifted from her grave,
> Set on your royal right hand. . . .
>
> [BT, 3–8]

These lines develop in *Time's Distractions* into the initial contrast between Arcadia and the world and furnish a reason for Desert's being in Arcadia. In the play, as in Chapman, peace depends upon a strong monarch who protects virtue. Chapman's metaphor,

> all Virtues,
> Summon'd with honour and with rich rewards
> To be her handmaids), . . .
>
> [BT, 8–10]

is made concrete in the characterizations of Virtue, Honor, and Desert. Similarly, Cupid's report in Chapman of the reconciliation of the two virtues Sophrosyne (Chastity) and Dapsile (Lib-

40

erality) develops in the play into a dialogue between Virtue and Fortune concerning their reconciliation for different reasons. In the masque, Cupid loses his bow and arrows to one of the virtues. She accidently shoots the other, who then

> did instantly repent all parts
> She play'd in urging that effeminate war,
> Lov'd and submitted; which submission
> This took so well that now they both are one;
> And as for your dear love [the king's] their
>   discords grew,
> So for your love they did their loves renew.
>
> [BT, 55–60]

The idea conveyed by these lines of discord resolved into harmony through the power of love and sustained by loving submission to the monarch is developed in *Time's Distractions* into its major themes and, hence, its action.

Like most of Chapman's tragedies, *Byron's Tragedy* explores political decay, as in its very different way does this play. In the main plot of *Byron's Tragedy* the core of sedition and corruption in the kingdom is Byron's inner corruption, his dreams of absolute power and his envy of the king. As the kingdom must finally purge itself of Byron to restore harmony, so in the play Time must be purged of those evils which cause division and discontent in Arcadia. It must have seemed to the author of *Time's Distractions* that Parliament was making real that which Byron desired:

> We must reform and have a new creation
> Of state and government, and on our Chaos
> Will I sit brooding up another world.
> I, who through all the dangers that can siege
> The life of man have forc'd my glorious way
> To the repairing of my country's ruins,
> Will ruin it again to re-advance it.
>
> [BT, 1.2.29–35]

Akin to a moral play, *Byron's Tragedy* pits Byron against the king, and the masque which the anonymous author used couples

41

justice and harmony with the ruler, a coupling which the action of Chapman's play reinforces.

Of the lines directly adapted from Chapman (*TD*, 215–252; *BT*, 2.20–51) only two trivial phrases are identical: "she answered note for note, relish for relish" and "from tree to tree." While the playwright follows the direction of Chapman's lines quite closely, he inserts others necessary for his purpose and eliminates some of Chapman's. The changes he makes in the verse, with its expansion of Chapman's compacted imagery, tend to move it closer to prose, but the passage remains lyrical:

> She smil'd at first, and sweetly shadow'd me
> With soft protection of her silver hand;
> Sometimes she tied my legs in her rich hair,
> And made me (past my nature, liberty)
> Proud of my fetters. As I pertly sat,
> On the white pillows of her naked breasts,
> I sung for joy. . . .
>
> [*BT*, 27–31]

> She smiled on me, called me her pretty bird
> And for her sport she tied my little legs
> In her fair hair. Proud of my golden fetters,
> I chirped for joy. She, confident of my tameness,
> Soon disentangled me and then she perched me
> Upon her naked breast. There being ravished,
> I sung with all my cheer and best of skill.
>
> [*TD*, 220–226]

Unfortunately, little of the verse in the rest of this play compares with the passage imitated from Chapman.

There is no reason to connect Chapman with this play, as J. D. Jump suggested one should, except as an important source.[52] Aside from the one image of the blackthorn which the playwright adapts from *Byron's Tragedy*, the other parallel lines which Jump finds in Chapman's works are either too common to be considered a direct source, or they have a more likely origin. Jump, for example, finds a parallel between the play's

[52] Jump, "The Anonymous Masque," p. 191.

42

The World
Is out of frame; disorder governs it,
Threatening to turn it all again to chaos

and Chapman's "The world's out of frame" (*Caesar and Pompey*,
2.1.38) and "all things now . . . Are turn'd to chaos" ("The
Shadow of Night," *Poems*, p. 4b). The parallel with the meaning
of the second quotation is somewhat distorted by its being taken
out of context, and closer similarities to the play's lines exist elsewhere. The satirical pamphlet by John Taylor quoted earlier, for
example, contains the lines "The world's turn'd upside downe,
from bad to worse, / Quite out of frame, *The Cart before the
Horse*," and all recall Shakespeare's "But let the frame of things
disjoint, both the worlds suffer" (*Macbeth*, 3.3.16).

Jump cites Chapman's line "danger haunts desert when he is
greatest" (*BT*, 5.4.226) as the source for the relationship between
Danger and Desert in the play, which it may have been. I believe it much more likely, however, that here the author followed
Spenser's Temple of Venus scene, Canto 10 of Book 4 in the
Faerie Queene. The allegory of *Time's Distractions* and the relationship between Love, Danger, and Desert both reflect so strongly the allegorical theme of this scene in the *Faerie Queene* that
it seems very likely that this canto is a direct source, not in its
language but, more significantly, in its conception. There are
many other echoes of Spenser's *Faerie Queene* in the play. The
introduction of Time into the Arcadian world recalls the Garden
of Adonis where

> . . . were it not, that Time their troubler is,
> All that in this delightfull gardin growes
> Should happy bee, and have immortall bliss . . . ,
> [3.6.41]

and the purgation of Time suggests familiarity with Error, who
"spewd out of her filthie maw / A floud of poyson horrible and
blacke" including "bookes and papers" (1.1.20). With her venomous vipers, Spenser's Envy, who with Detraction lets loose the
Blatant Beast (5.12.30ff.), has several characteristics in common
with Envy in *Time's Distractions*.

43

Because of the frequency with which such figures appear in the Renaissance, it is, nevertheless, difficult to make precise attributions. The figure of Envy who appears in the Induction to Jonson's *Poetaster* and elsewhere in Jonson's work also figures in Townshend's *Tempe Restored,* Dekker's *King's Entertainment* and *London Triumphing,* Middleton's *Triumphs of Truth,* and possibly a good many more. Juno appears as a queen in the masque in Shakespeare's *The Tempest* and in Jonson's *Hymenaei.* Sight and Search's description of Juno's entrance and the characters of the Clouds in *Time's Distractions* may, however, be a deliberate allusion to Jonson's masque, in which Juno entered most impressively:

> Here, the upper part of the Scene, which was all of
> Clouds, and made artifically to swell, and ride like
> the Racke, began to open; and, the ayre clearing, in the
> top thereof was discouered IUNO, sitting in a Throne,
> supported by two beautifull *Peacockes*; her attyre rich,
> and like a Queene . . . round about her sate the spirites
> of the ayre, in seuerall colours, making musique. . . .
>
> [*Hymenaei,* 212ff.]

In *Time's Distractions* Juno refers to the Clouds' entrance from "the region of the air" (1. 56) and alludes to a masque discovery scene; before the dance she charms "the air to give us music" (1. 137). On the other hand, it is in Shakespeare's masque that she is given supreme authority as "highest queen of state."

The natures of two characters in the play do, however, seem to be derived directly from Jonson. In *Cynthia's Revels* a character named Simplicity appears in the first of the masques "without folds, without pleights, without colour, without counterfeit: and (to speak plainly) *Plainenesse* it selfe," a description which serves as a fair statement of his role in the play. In the same play Virtue, usually represented as being young and beautiful, is "a poor Nymph . . . that's scarce able to buy her selfe a gowne" (Induction, 89ff.) just as she is in the play.

Because the imaginative quality of *Time's Distractions* arises from the way in which the author unified commonplace ideas and images to make a political statement relevant to his time, one is more likely to uncover analogues than sources. Whatever unknown works he may have drawn upon, it is certain that he was attracted to those which celebrate harmony and deprecate discord and which insist upon an order and degree predicated on the sovereign.

Textual Note

The following text has been prepared from folios 212–223 of British Museum MS. Egerton 1994. An analysis of the transcriber's errors, corrected and uncorrected, indicates that he was copying from another manuscript, one unlikely to have been his own. Haste in copying unfamiliar material explains his characteristic errors of picking up words or speech tags prematurely, lineating verse as prose, making incomplete corrections, repeating words or phrases, and erroneously anticipating the next word or line. The hand is probably not that of a professional scribe; letter formations are too irregular and spelling too inconsistent even for an age in which consistency is rare. The manuscript also shows evidence of the copyist's fatigue; errors increase as he approaches the end of acts and the conclusion of the play. The hand becomes looser and larger until on the last page the letters are triple or more the size of those at the beginning of act 5.

Although the handwriting remains the same and the text is clearly not a prompt copy, some of the stage directions throughout the play are almost certainly later additions. These generally serve to make more explicit the original direction, as, for example, at line 645, where the initial stage direction, "Exeunt, halting off," is centered, and to the right is the more detailed direction, "Dance, kick, and beat each other: exit."

If the play was performed, the transcriber was possibly one of the actors. Professional actors used only cue sheets, but amateurs required copies of the entire play, and this copy may have been

45

made for that purpose. On the other hand, the transcriber may simply have been a friend of the author who wanted a copy of the play. One cannot tell from the internal evidence alone.

For the modernized text which follows I have silently removed almost all of the original punctuation, substituting modern marks, expanded most contractions, and modernized all spelling. I have expanded the contracted forms of characters' names in speech prefixes and stage directions, and I have regularized the position of both and italicized them. Additions to the original are bracketed; conjectured readings of damaged or unclear portions of the manuscript are placed within parentheses. Other textual problems are footnoted. I have followed the lineation of the original.

Time's Distractions
Modernized Text

Nomina Actorum

Time	Juno
Age	Virtue
Will	Fortune
Judgment	Honor
Simplicity	Desert
Sight	Envy
Search	Suspicion
Danger	Clouds
Love	Malice
Satyrs	Jealousy

August 5th, 1643

47

Act I

Sight and Search.

Sight. Come, brother Search. While our masters
        are away and their flocks   1
        in our charge are grazing,[1] we may here
        look about us.
Search. True, brother Sight. Thy delight is upon
        the present objects—
        the hills, the springs, the rivers, groves,
        the lawns, the meadows
        with all the pleasant fruits and flowers of
        this earthly paradise,   5
        Arcadia. But, Sight, you are but a superficial
        surveyor and only
        feast your eye with those outward delights;
        I, mine intellect with the
        healthfulness of the air, the wholesomeness
        of the food, the
        condition of the people, the love, the peace,
        the amity that
        flows here and only here in all the
        world. Here content   10
        lives in the free enjoyment of all her own
        without fear of
        rapine and oppression. Here's no wrong done.
        Here Virtue lives; here, unpunished.
Sight. Virtue? Does she live here, too?
Search. Alas, poor lady, she's compelled to do it.
        Such is the alchemy   15
        of the age abroad that it contents itself
        with a visor of virtue
        without substance. Only this kingdom is
        her sanctuary against

---

[1] The phrase *and their flocks* is repeated in the MS.

48

	the spite of all the world. She is my	
	master's mistress.	
Sight.	Well, Search, thou servest a discreet	
	master and learnest much of him.	
	His name is Judgment and [he] seldom	
	errs. My master's name is	20
	Will. Thou knowest he's often rash, but	
	sometimes in the right.	
Search.	He's much beholding to my master, then,	
	for his company to	
	direct him. Will without Judgment goes	
	much astray. And they are	
	both well fitted with helpful servants,	
	for thou that are Sight servest Will	
	and showest him all his objects, and I	
	that am Search serve Judgment	25
	for his direction.	
Sight.	But both our services are equal to 'em;	
	both, indeed.	
Search.	Right. Where the masters are entire	
	friends, their servants are in common	
	with 'em—and so much upon that subject.	
	When sawest thy master Will's	
	mistress? Has he achieved her yet?	30
Sight.	Who? Mistress Desert?	
Search.	Who else, I prithee? She is the only one;	
	she seeks and follows	
	into this kingdom, as my master has done,	
	dame Virtue.	
Sight.	I would they both had their desires on them,	
	but I see Danger at the heels	
	of one of those ladies and Envy at the	
	other's, and those two mischiefs are	35
	enough to infect or destroy the peace of	
	this blissful Arcadia,	

49

	which all the world, being weary of the	
	troubles and spoils of their	
	own nations, seeks to inhabit.	
Search.	For that, Sight, you must look afore you,	
	and I search round about into [it].	
	So must our masters, too. Whither are they	
	gone today?	40
Sight.	They are gone a fishing with old Simpli-	
	city, the fisherman, to recreate	
	their tedious love thoughts— But what	
	was my fear that mortals sh(all)	
	find disquiet here when the gods begin to	
	make their entrance? See, Se(arch)—	
	Juno descending with her Clouds about her.	
	Oh that our masters saw this s(ight)!	
Search.	It is not strange. This kingdom is so	
	happy that the gods do of(ten) d(escend)	45
	and here converse with mortals. Now she	
	is landed with her fantastic	
	women, the Clouds.	

Enter Juno, 2 or 3 Clouds.

Cloud.	Juno, great queen, we that have been	
	your chariot	
	In your de(scent) from your heavenly	
	palace	
	———— to be your	
	f(ollow)er,[2]	50
	Nymphlike to wait upon your sovereignty	
	On these Arcadian hills, whence you may	
	view	
	The fruitful valleys and the pleasant	
	plains,	
	To which the only happy of the world	
	Have wisely from the world retired themselves	55
	To live in safety and to die in peace.	

[2] Much of this line is unreadable in the MS.

Juno.	I called you from your region of the air	
	That so heaven's curtains being drawn	
	I might	
	Better discover what is done beneath,	
	And as I cast mine eye upon the world,	60
	I behold Fortune flying over all	
	The kingdoms of the earth, making at last	
	Her way into this part as spying Virtue.[3]	

Enter Fortune, Virtue

2d Clo.	They hasten towards you.	
Juno.	I conceive the cause.	65
	Fortune has need of Virtue now to move	
	A suit to me, else I should wonder at	
	Her nimble flight, she being now so great	
	A burden to herself.	
1st Clo.	She appears big, indeed.	70
Juno.	She's great with child.	
1st Clo.	I have heard she was always barren.	
Juno.	'Tis true the gods to plague the idleness	
	And the ingratitude of men had shut	
	Her womb and made her so. Maugre,[4] it haps	75
	She now is near her time and seeks my aid	
	For her delivery.	
1st Clo.	They are in deep conference.[5]	
Juno.	Let us walk by.	
Fortune.	Virtue, whatever long contention	80
	Hath severed us, now let it die forgotten	
	Upon your perfect reconciliation.	
Virtue.	When we strove most against each other,	
	Our works were very like. We both	
	advanced,	
	We both enriched, both honored men at	
	pleasure.	85

[3] Read *as she spies Virtue.*
[4] In the MS. *maugre* reads *mow bre.*
[5] In the MS. *conference* reads *oonffesence.*

51

Fortune.	And when our favors have been in their spring,
	Ready to bud forth, we have been delighted
	To exercise those men like to the blackthorn,
	Which puts his leaf out with most bitter storms.
Virtue.	See where the goddess walks to whom we must prefer the suit?
Juno.	Fortune and Virtue, I rejoice to find you in such amity together here.
	What news abroad upon the earth?
Virtue.	The world
	Is out of frame; disorder governs it,
	Threatening to turn it all again to chaos.
	Poor I am, banished from all parts but this,
	And therein am yet happy. Here I live,
	Untrod upon, free from the violence
	Of rage and cruelty, pride, and ignorance.
	The great do not oppress 'cause I am poor,
	Nor the poor curse because I give no more.
	When I had wealth and power, all would not do.
	Here innocence maintains and guards me, too.
[Juno.]	Poor Virtue. Wert thou banished?
[Virtue.]	(I w)ent away
	On pain of present death, or to have starved,
	If longer I remained.
Juno.	But how came Fortune to leave those parts of the world?
Fortune.	I was so much dishonored in my gifts
	Of wealth and peace, prosperity, and plenty
	Which I bestowed on that ungrateful world,
	When I saw all perverted or abused
	To ruin or demolish with my means,

90

95

100

105

110

52

	Where they ought rather to repair and build,	
	To breed unnatural strife and bloody wars	115
	To the destructions of the populous nations	

Where they ought rather to repair and
    build,
To breed unnatural strife and bloody wars   115
To the destructions of the populous nations
With that which I bestowed to be their
    glories,
I could no longer with my Honor stay,
But took my swiftest wings and fled away.

Juno.   You could no longer with your Honor stay?   120
Fortune, I now perceive the charge you
    carry
Within you. Thou art great with Honor,
    Fortune,
And it shall prove the happiest birth that
    ever
Arcadia was blest with. I myself
Will, as I am Lucina, be thy midwife   125
And safe deliver thee thy birth of Honor.

Fortune.   Here Fortune then hangs up her wings and
    breaks
Her turning wheel, with purpose never to
    Depart out of Arcadia.

Juno.   'Tis well.   130
I see thy time approach, but by my power
And Virtue's help, with these my shadowing
    Clouds,
I'll pluck one feather from Time's wings
    or borrow
Out of your urgent haste two or three
    minutes
To try our feet on this Arcadian grass   135
In a soft measure for our welcome hither,
Thus charming first the air to give us music.
                               Dance.

Juno.   Come, Fortune, here you're safe. The greedy
    world,

Which you have passed, would have ripped
    up your womb
To anticipate your fruit ere it was ripe,   140
Like to those dunghill scarabs that pursued
The eagle for her eggs which Jupiter
For the more safety let be lain in his lap,
You upon Juno's knees shall be delivered.

Virtue.   And happy thou, Arcadia, when 'tis said,   145
    Juno in thee herself a midwife made.

[Search.]   Come away, Sight. All this shall to our
    masters.

Finis Actus Primi

Act II

Sight and Search.

Sight.   What a sight have we seen! Fortune with
    child and come to
    be delivered in Arcadia. A thousand to
    one her belly is
    full of town[s], towers, castles, churches,
    honors, offices, crow(n)s,   150
    and (k)ingdoms. The store of all the
    world will now be ours.

Search.   Winter is gone. Let our flocks dance. We
    shall have continual summer.

Sight.   Avant curds and cheesecakes! We will now
    change our diet
    and make feasts for all comers.

Search.   We'll send to all the hospitals in the
    world for all the   155
    lame soldiers that have got nothing by
    service but wounds and
    diseases.

Sight.	Call out every poor priest, too, which is beaten so small
	between two terrible millstones, subsidy and sacrilege, that he
	hath not oatmeal to put in his porridge. 160
Search.	Charge every lawyer to break his angle and fish no more
	for causes. Here they may live honestly and follow Virtue.
Sight.	While thou speak it of fishing, we are arrived where our masters
	are a fishing— But let us not mind 'em yet.

Enter Will, Judgment, Simplicity pulling
a net; two or three to help.

Judgment.	Call for more help. We are not able to draw the net a land. 165
Will.	See, some of our servants. Sight and Search, come hither quickly and help.
Search.	Arcadia is now wealthier than ever it was.
Will.	Villains, why stir you not? What is your wonder there?
Sight.	O, master, this year is enough to make every knave in the cards
	a king; therefore, you are made and we are all made master. 170
Judg.	You are mad, are you not? What is the matter?
Sight.	Our very sheep shall dance more courtly than the damoisel of France.
Judg.	What is the reason of your jollity?
Search.	Juno is come down from heaven to bless Arcadia, and Fortune
	has forsaken all the nations of the earth to enrich Arcadia. Virtue 175
	is only here; Desert is here. What would you have more?

Judg.	Is Fortune arrived here, dost say?
Search.	Yes, great with child to grace this
	kingdom with her issue. Juno
	has brought her abed by this time. The
	gods make quick work, you know.
Sight.	And Fortune has hanged up her wings here
	and broke her 180
	wheel here. See where the pieces lie
	here?
Simpl.	My heart gave me we should have good
	luck. Sure her coming
	hither hath so filled my net that without
	more help we shall never draw it (in).
Search.	Alas, poor Simplicity, thy share will be
	least when we fall to scrambli(ng).
Will.	Come, everyone, set hands to the cords and
	pull all together. 185
All.	Huwa, huva-ho! Huva hoot!
Sight.	Huppa! 'tis come! We have it!
Search.	I think it be a porpoise.
Will.	Take it out, fisherman.
Search.	It looks like a conger. 'Tis somewhat
	gray. 190
[Simpl.]	I think all the world will come either by
	sea or land.
	Cupid taken out of the net.
Simpl.	Alas, we are undone.
Cupid.	Presumptuous wretches! How dare you draw
	me out of my bed and break my sleep?
Simpl.	What art thou? Speak in the name of
	Neptune, Pisces, and Aquarius.
	Speak! What art thou? 195
[Cupid.]	Have you lived to these years and yet
	know not Love?
Will, Judg., Simpl.	Love?

Search.	Cupid!
Sight.	Great god, oh, little mighty! None but
	your weight could have laden
	our net so, nor any but your hot divinity
	could have held out water, 200
	as you have done, to lie in the sea and
	no wet upon you.
Cupid.	The sea is my bed wherein my mother
	Venus was born, and there
	I laid me down to sleep with purpose so
	to hide myself
	forever from the eyes of men.
[Will.]	Sweet Love, what moved you to it? 205
Love.	A fair nymph in Arcadia was the cause.
[Will.]	Which of them? Here are many.
[Love.]	(Bu)t she's the fairest, and her name,
	Desert.
[Will.]	(S)he is my mistress.
Love.	I knew it, Will, and, trust me, 'twas for
	thee, 210
	Thy only sake, that I have undergone
	this.
	Attend my story, Will, Judgment, and the
	rest.
Sight.	His little mightyship knows us all. But
	while he tells his story,
	we'll spread the news of his arrival.
	Exit Sight, Search, Simplicity.
Love.	For thy sake, Will, I feathered all my
	thoughts 215
	And in a bird's shape flew into her bosom,
	The bosom of Desert, thy beauteous mistress,
	As if I had been driven by the hawk
	In that sweet sanctuary to save my life.
	She smiled on me, called me her pretty bird, 220

57

And for her sport she tied my little legs
In her fair hair. Proud of my golden
   fetters,
I chirped for joy. She, confident of my
   tameness,
Soon disentangled me, and then she perched me
Upon her naked breast. There, being ravished,   225
I sung with all my cheer and best of skill.
She answered note for note, relish for
   relish,
And ran division with such art and ease
That she exceeded me.

Judg.   There was rare music.   230

Love.   In this sweet strife, forgetting where I
   stood,
I trod so hard in straining of my voice
That with my claw I rent her tender skin,
Which as she felt and saw vermilion follow,
Staining the color of Adonis bleeding   235
In Venus' lap, with indignation she cast me
   from her.

Will.   That fortune be to all that injure her.

Love.   Then I put on this shepherd's shape you see
And took my bow and quiver as in revenge
Against the birds, shooting and following
   them   240
From tree to tree. She, passing by, beheld
And liked the sport. I offered her my prey,
Which she received and asked to feel my bow,
Which when she handled and beheld the beauty
Of my bright arrows, she began to beg 'em.   245
I answered they were all my riches; yet,
I was content to hazard all and stake 'em
Down to a kiss at a game at chess with her.
"Wanton," quoth she, being privy to her
   skill,

"A match." Then she with that dexterity 250
Answered my challenge that I lost my
   weapons.[6]
Now Cupid's shafts are headed with her looks.
My mother, soon perceiving my disgrace—
My arms being lost and gone which made me
   a terror
To all the world—she took away my wings, 255
Renounced me for her child, and cast me
   from her,
And more to be revenged upon Desert,
Commanded Danger to be her strong keeper,
That should she empt' my quiver at the
   hearts
Of men, they might not dare to court her,
   fearing 260
That horrid mischief that attends her.
On this I threw me headlong on the sea
To sleep my time out in the bottom of it,
Whence you have pulled me up to be a scorn
To all the world. 265

Will.   Not so, my pretty boy. I'll arm thee again.
My breast shall be thy quiver; my sighs, thy
   shafts.
And here's an opportunity to be winged again.
   See here, the wings of Fortune.

[Love.]   Fortune's wings
Are full of giddy feathers, too unsure 270
For me to fly withal. But I will stay with
   you,
I like so well this air. Only you must
Provide to keep me from the hands of Danger
T(h)at waits upon Desert.

Will.   Ourselves and all 275

---

[6] Read *such dexterity* for *that dexterity*.

Arcadia shall be your guard,[7] and where
Love passes and resides, he shall be always
Armed and attended by a band of lovers,
      Enter Sight, Search, Simplicity,
        Swains, Nymphs to dance.
Such faithful ones as if that ugly Danger
Were Lucifer himself, they should defend you.   280
See, Sight and Search have raised the country
  already
And brought the swains and nymphs to wait on
  Love.

Sight.   Come away, lads and lasses,
      And wheresoever Love passes
        Let us his guard and followers be.
    Since he doth grace our plains,
      Let all the nymphs and swains   285
        With dances and with melody
    Surround his person in a ring,
      Crowning his deity our king.
                           Dance.

Will.   Majesty, Fortune, Virtue, Love,
    This day do in Arcadia move.[8]
    What more addition or increase   290
    Need we to keep us here in peace?

Judg.   Yes, Will, we must not be so confident,
    Nor yet presume upon our peace or safety.
        Enter Desert with a bow and quiver;
          Danger following.

Will.   Not when Desert herself, my divine mistress,
    Makes towards us.   295

Love.   But see who follows her! I must away.

Will.   Stay, gentle Love.

Love.   Not in the face of Danger.
                           Exit.

[7] In the MS. *and all* is repeated.
[8] In the MS. *Arcadia* reads *Arrabia.*

Sight.	Sight dares not take a glimpse of him.
	Exit.
Search.	The more Search looks on him, the worse
	he likes him.
	Exit.
Simpl.	He has been my companion at sea, but I dare
	not look on him ashore.
	Exit.
Will.	Villains, do you all leave your masters at
	the sight of Danger?
	Good Judgment, do not you leave me.
Judg.	If you stay here, I must, but for this once
	I will not leave you
	But force you from this place.
	Desert this time by you must be deserted.
Will.	Was ever happy peace so soon perverted?
	Exit [Judgment and Will].
Desert.	Monster, why dost not leave me?
Danger.	Not 'til you lay down those arms.
Desert.	I would Love had 'em again. I find their
	weight
	Too ponderous for Desert to carry, attended
	by thy stern cruelty.
Danger.	I must and will attend you for your guard.
	I hurt not you, but stand up for a terror
	To all that shall approach or dare to court
	you.
	You are my charge. "Keep off from due
	Desert,"
	I speak to all the world.
Desert.	Thou art but a boisterous fool and canst
	fright none
	That's armed with perfect resolution.
Danger.	Am a fool?
Desert.	Yes, to the truly valiant.
Danger.	Yet I have stood between two mighty armies

305

310

315

320

61

And made them both retreat without a battle
At the mere sight of me. And when at sea
I list to cool myself upon a rock,
I make whole fleets of warlike ships strike
    sail   325
Or pass aloof. Nay, when I am at feasts,
Banquets, and revels—in the midst of all
Delights and royalties of powers and states—
My very shadow can disperse and force them
To forsake all and fly from Danger's
    presence.   330

Desert.   I do conjure thee: leave me.

Danger.   In vain you urge it. Take which way you can,
I will not be a step behind you.

Desert.   Oh, Love, where art thou? Take again thy
    arms.

Danger.   Love hears you not.   335

Desert.   Juno, Fortune, Virtue! O you great powers—
Will none vouchsafe to rescue due Desert?

Danger.   Haugh, haugh, haugh. My laughter is thy
    smart.

Exeunt.
Finis Actus Secundi

Act III

Enter Time.

Time.   Happy and blest Arcadia! How glad
And merry grows old Time here in thy confines   340
To see the plenty in a flourishing peace
That flows and spreads itself through all
    this nation.
Only methought I saw a glimpse of Danger
           Enter Security.
Pass through my walks, attending on Desert.

Secur.	It startled me a little, but I tell you,	345
	It was not Danger. Be fearless, Time, and	
	careless.	
Time.	My sweet and lovely friend, Security,	
	I will not think upon him, but rely	
	Upon thy word. My sweet Security,	
	Most soft and gentle nymph, my only	
	mistress,	350
	Thy sweet embrace has cast a slumber on me,	
	In which old restless Time will rest awhile,	
	In spite of Danger.	

He falls asleep.

| Secur. | Do so while I make sweeter thy soft sleep. |

Song.

Enter Envy, Suspicion, Necessity, 5 or 6
hags more.

[Secur.]	Envy and all her brood! Poor Time, I must	
	no longer guard thee;	355
	I cannot have a biding among these.	

Exit.

Envy.	Security has played her part and lulled	
	old Time asleep. The	
	reverend gentleman is waxed a wanton and	
	given to dalliance is he.	
	But we will fit. Come away, Suspicion.	
	Come, Necessity. Come,	
	Jealousy and Fear, Spite, Mischief, Rancor,	
	Malice—all the	360
	whole brood of you. Come apace, Suspicion;	
	thou art too fearful.	
Susp.	Envy, thou hast undone me to carry me so far	
	from my strong castle,	
	when I cannot but tremble and startle	
	at every step.[9]	

[9] In the MS. *and* reads *at.*

Envy.	I'll set thee safe again into thy rock when
	we have done our work. 365
Susp.	What work is that, or wherefore come we
	hither?
[Envy.]	To infect the sweet tranquility of Arcadia,

The only part of the world that hath
    been free
From the effects of our malignancy; to cross
    the intents of Fortune and dame Virtue,
Who, to avoid my vipers that do crawl
Upon all other kingdoms of the earth, 370
Are come to inhabit here, as if this land
Were not by Envy to be found. Here Fortune
Is a glad mother of a gallant daughter
Called Honor, who was nursed and bred by
    Virtue,
And in a little time grown to that stature 375
By this Arcadia's peace that she is ready,
Or will be, for a husband very shortly,
If we bestir us not. Come, while Time sleeps,
Dreaming of dull Security, his mistress,
Let's work our charms into his heart and
    brains 380
To infuse distraction in him. First,
    Suspicion,
Lay thy cold hand upon his heart, while I
To his ears and eyes my vipers thus apply.
Come, Jealousy, Fear, Spite, Malice, and
    the rest,
And in your offices do all your best. 385
Forget not you, Necessity, to nip him,
And let none of our mischiefs overslip him.
But laugh and dance to think how mad he'll be,
And all Arcadia, as mad as he.
Dance.

Envy.   Time, when thou wakest thou, it shall not
        appear   390
        That Envy with her viperous brood was here;
        Yet by the frantic arts the world shall see,
        Time sleeps not safely with Security.
                        Exit [all but Time].
                        Time awakes.
Time.   What cold is this within me? Where's
        Security?
        Fled from me? I am not safe, then; no,
        nor well.   395
        But who or what am I? Sure I was Time,
        And am and must be Time, but strangely
        altered.
        How light and jocund was I ere I slept,
        And what a world of strange diseases ran
        Through all my vitals. Now Time is grown   400
        Full of corruption, full of vice and
        mischief.
        Envy, Suspicion, Malice, and Revenge,
        Methinks, flow in me; yet for what, I
        know not.
        And I so late applaud and glorify
        Arcadia because Desert lived here,[10]   405
        Will, Judgment, Fortune, Virtue, Love,
        and Honor.
        I'll now become a scourge unto them all
        And poison all their glories. Thou Arcadia,
        That sufferest Time to be abused in 's sleep,
        Upon thy earth shall feel my whips and be   410
        Punished in him as he's abused by thee.
        Here I'll begin to scatter my infection.[11]

[10] Read *applauded* and *glorified.*
[11] In the MS. *infection* reads *iffection.*

Enter Age like a hermit; Love
in his former habit.

Age. And is this true, my boy? Thou tellest
  me that
  Thou didst discover Danger in Arcadia
  And ranst into my cell for safety?   415

Love. And for your service, too, sir.

Age. Art thou quite friendless, sayest thou?

Love. A poor, fatherless child, sir. You shall
  find me diligent.

Age. I like the quickness of thine, be it not
  a little too wanton.

Love. I am yet but a child, sir. Age will bridle it.   420

Age. [*Aside*] What a child's answer there was. [*To Love*]
  True, my boy.
  If you be idle, I shall curb you and see
  that you
  Observe nothing but Age and Virtue.

Time. [*Aside*] That shall Time quickly try. [*To Age*] Sir,
  by your leave,
  May not Time pass by you?   425

Age. O Time, thou hast trod upon my foot. Dost
  give me warning?

Love. 'Tis but a love trick, master; fear it not.

Time. Tell me, what art thou?

Age. Thou knowest I am Age and made old by thee.
  My cell is here at hand, where I intend   430
  To spend my days in contemplation of Virtue,
  whom I serve.

[*Time.*] I pray thee, tell me, Age, is any danger in
  sleeping hereabout?
  Does any venomous vermin or enchantress
  haunt these places?

[*Age.*] Time does but try me. Here are no such
  things.

66

	You know it, Time; nothing than you is wiser.
	You can discuss 435
	All secrets. Take counsel of yourself, and
	you cannot err.
	But I can boast [that] Arcadia for health
	And happiness is earth's only paradise.
	Age is no burden here unto itself.
Time.	Think thyself young again, then. The boy
	that follows thee 440
	can make thee so. There's a blast of my
	infection for thee!

Exit.

Age.	What has Time done to me, boy?
Love.	Sir—
Age.	Come hither, boy.
Love.	Here, Sir. 445
Age.	O, Time, what hast thou done? Why? Boy, I say!
Love.	Here, Sir. I am here.
Age.	Most strange. How is Age metamorphosed on a sudden? Was not I Age but now? Come hither. Come hither!
Love.	What say you, sir? 450
Age.	Wilt thou not come, boy? Come, boy.
Love.	[Aside] The old man dotes outright. Or, can he call and neither see nor hear me? [To Age] Here, sir. Here, sir.
Age.	O, boy. Boy. Boy! Boy! Boy! Come nearer me.
Love.	What is your will, sir? 455
Age.	Canst thou perceive any white hairs upon me?
Love.	No, not a white hair about you, sir, but only on your head and face.
Age.	Are any there? You will not lie. Fetch me my bowl of water, Or—tarry sirrah—I'll make me a looking glass of your eyes.

Love.	Pray do not break 'em, sir, if you should
	chance to dislike
	your own looks.
Age.	The truest glass that ever was inspected.
	It represents my perfect knowledge to me.
	I know my hair was lovely, brown as berry.
	I know my lips and cheeks were a red cherry.
	A ha, my boy, thine eyes are perfect mirrors.
Love.	[*Aside*] What heretics are they, then, that say love
	is blind.
Age.	But you have a false tongue, sirrah. You
	said I was white. Are
	these hairs white? I'll untongue you, boy,
	unless you do me
	present service. What a strange, youthful
	tickling do I feel.
Love.	Any service, master.
Age.	Go fetch me a wench.
Love.	What to do, master?
Age.	What but to do! You knave, run fetch me an
	able and a delightful one.
Love.	Are you in earnest, sir?
Age.	Is Age a liar, thinkst thou?
Love.	O, sir, old Age may by authority outlie new
	books. But master,
	to what country must I travel for a glib bit
	for you that
	will go down without chewing? I mean, a
	wench that will be won
	without wooing. All the nymphs and lasses
	in Arcadia are too virtuous.
	Oh, by your own late example, 'twas your
	profession and you did but now
	instruct and charge me to follow Virtue only.
	"A wench," quoth a. I might
	as soon find one in England as here.

Line numbers in right margin: 460, 465, 470, 475, 480

Enter Juno, Fortune, Virtue
and Honor.

	But master, what say you to	
	these? Here be fine knickknacks for you,	
	if you can get their good wills.	485
Age.	Oh, I was almost lost. Time had almost	
	transformed me into a beast,	
	but the mere sight of those divinities	
	hath recollected reason to my sense,	
	which now I'll hold.	
Love.	That's as please Time and me.[12]	
Age.	Hail, sacred deities.	490
	Great Juno, Fortune, Virtue, late-born Honor,	
	Grown to a height which shows the influence	
	By which she was conceived, a generation flow-	
	ing from the gods.	
[Juno.]	Honor, I welcome thee into the world.	
	As thou art born descended of the gods,	495
	Thy (hon)or may inform thee to subdue	
	Those monsters which invade the unbridled	
	youth	
	Of human race.[13] Yet, to avoid the trams	
	And slippery paths of Envy, which are laid	
	To make thee slip or fall, be sure to have	500
	An eye to Virtue here that nursed thee. She	
	Can better help thee in thy ways than Fortune,	
	Although thy mother. And now, Age, I'll tell	
	thee,	
	Our coming was to revel in your bower.	
Age.	Age is made happy in it.	505
Juno.	What boy is this you keep? Have I not seen	
	him?	
Love.	[*Aside*] You shall not know me now, my good aunt.	

---

[12] Read *as will* for *as*.
[13] The conjectured *honor* could possibly be *power*.

69

Age.	A pretty, witty wag. I lately entertained him.
	Question him, good madam, if you please.
Juno.	My boy, which of all us wouldst choose to be thy mistress? 510
Love.	Master, which do you like best? You wanted a wench even now.
Age.	No more o' that. No more o' that, good boy.
Juno.	Answer me, boy.
Love.	You madam, if you'll be. My master's wife must be my mistress. My
	service must attend upon his choice. But I have heard him call you Juno, 515
	and I have been told of one of that name that is the supremest scold
	that ever tipped nectar over a tongue. He shall have none of you
	for name's sake.
Juno.	What a boy's this! I am answered.
Fortune.	What sayst to me, my lad? 520
Love.	Oh, lady Fortune, my master is a slayed man. You are too fickle and no
	housewife for him. You are here today and gone tomorrow.
Virtue.	Shall I have your election?
Love.	I could like you well, dame Virtue, for the good that is within you,
	but you have so little without you that I know not what a man of the 525
	world should do with you except to beg withal.
Honor.	What think you of me, sir?
Love.	You, my lady Honor, would make a good match for an old man because
	Age is, or should be, honorable, but had I been of counsel with your

	midwife, you should never have been born here	
	in Arcadia.	530
Honor.	Why, I prithee?	
Love.	Because you will tyrannize over all our ease	
	and ride the liberty	
	Of love with a rough bit. 'Twas merry in	
	Arcadia when gloves,	
	Scarfs, garters, chains, and ribbons passed	
	Fearless and freely and were worn for favors,	535
	When nymphs and shepherds tumbled without	
	check	
	Upon the flowery banks, or, changing kisses,	
	ladies	
	Laid their breasts open like a bed of lilies	
	For love to sleep in. Lovers, too, might	
	touch	
	To try which is the softest, and every amorous	540
	Demand was answered with "If you will, you may."	
	These golden days are gone. Honor is stern,	
	Strict, full of doubts, denials, taunts,	
	repulses.	
	She casts a cover over nature's riches	
	To hide them from the sight of men and ties	545
	The tresses of the hair up in pure order,	
	Which used to wave and flourish in the wind.	
	And to demands which heretofore were easy,	
	Women say now, "I cannot with my honor."	
Juno.	You bid us question him, Age, and he questions	
	us, methinks.	550
Honor.	You are a wanton wag and would be whipped.	
[Love.]	Did I not tell you what Honor was? How she	
	threatens already!	
Virtue.	What a strange, unheard-of boy, this.	
Juno.	I have not known his like but Cupid's self.	
	But let him pass. We do not what we came for,	555
	To grace old Age's bower with a measure.	

71

	Come, you can talk, sir. Can you dance as well?
Love.	If Honor will permit me, I will try.
Juno.	Well, we shall find in time, sir, what you are.
	And, Age, be lively now and jump with us.
Age.	I am inspired to do so.

560

Dance.
In the midst of the dance,
Time enters.

Time.	[*Aside*] Are you so merry? I'll make one among you to mar the sport.

Time dances 'til on a sudden
they stop amazedly.

Juno.	Stay. Here's one more than our number.
Virtue.	'Tis Time. How has he overtaken us?
Fortune.	How madly he looks. Surely, he's much distracted.

565

Time.	No more than I will make you, all over whom my power may be prevalent.
Juno.	I am above thy spite.
Time.	But all the rest and all Arcadia
	Shall feel the change of Time. And thus I spread
	The infection I have taken here among you.

570

Juno.	Away! Let's fly from him.
Fortune, Virtue, Honor.	Agh! Agh! Away, agh!
Age.	My fit's upon me again. I must follow the females.
	" 'Stay, nymph; stay, nymph,' cried Apollo."

And exit, singing.

Love.	I feel a change in myself. O, cursed Time!

575

[Time.]	Ha, ha, ha. Time has been poisoned here and where the time
	O'erflows with venom, that o'erwhelms the clime.

Finis Actus Tertii

72

Act IV

Enter Time below, Juno above.

Time.   Ha, ha, ha. My spleen is tickled, while my
      rancor flies
      Through all this nation where I took infection.
      Here will I sit and note the passages   580
      Of their vexation in my revenge.

Juno.   Juno is yet above thee, Time, and by
      Her power will protect Arcadia
      From a perversion. Although she suffer
      Yet for a while thy wild distractions   585
      To trouble and afflict them, I will free
      Them from thy scourge at last and temper thee.

Enter Judgment and Will.

Time.   Judgment and Will together by the ears.

Will.   I will no more endure thee.

Judg.   Nor I, thee. Rash, giddy fool, forsake my
      company,   590
      or I will hurl thee into oblivion.

Will.   Judgment, thou canst not will. Will be
      predominant
      when Judgment shall be thrust out of his
      office.

Judg.   When Judgment shall not pass on the foolhardy,
      thou thine own neck shall break. Go to thy
      ruin.   595

Exit.

Will.   Go, profound Judgment. Choke thyself with
      pebbles in the bottom of the sea.

Exit.

Time.   Ha, ha, ha. Two old friends parted.

Juno.   I shall reunite them by divine power, or Time
      must not continue.

Time.   Who be the next? Oh, Sight and Search. Ha,
      ha, ha.

73

Search.	Sight, I will dig out thine eyes.	600
Sight.	Search, I will tear out thine entrails.	
Search.	I'll spoil your hare finding.	
Sight.	And I, thy gold finding. Away, Jakes farmer. Faugh.	
Search.	If thou keepest thine eyes, thou shalt be accursed with 'em, for thou shalt use them for nothing but in setting for sergeants.	605
Sight.	If thou keepest thy quality of searching, it shall be for nothing but intelligences for some weak statesman that shall for thy reward at last be sure to hang thee.	
Search.	Or, dost hear? thou shalt be bound 'prentice to a spectacle maker that shall shoot thee through a perspective glass into the chamber window of some naked courtesan who shall, with a trick that she will show thee, strike thee blind.	610
Sight.	Thou shalt first belong to some perpetual constable that shall carry thee by warrant into the lodging of some malefactor that shall dash thy brains out.	

Enter Simplicity.

Simpl.	What are you wording out? Oh, do you but scold and threaten one another, you poor-spirited, hen-hearted rascals?	615
Time.	A delicate madness! Simplicity itself grown the roaringest boy of 'em all. He has forgot to profess his simple judgment and to talk of fish.	
Simpl.	Can you not fight when all the shepherds in Arcadia have broke their oars,	

74

	hooks, and tar boxes in an unknown quarrel?	
	Time has set 'em by the ears, they say.	
Time.	Ha, ha, ha.	620
Simpl.	A word and a blow, you slaves, a word and a	
	blow. To it and to it roundly, or by	
	the soul of Simplicity, I'll beat you both.	
Sight.	Away, poor fool, which truly for your part	
	and in simple judgment.[14]	
Simpl.	I hate those words at this time.	
Search.	Away, away. Go fish; go fish.	625
[Simpl.]	I hate the name of fishing. Give me flesh	
	and fighting. Will you fight, or be pric(ked)	
	in the breech to it? Poor underhearted wretches,	
	you. Fight, you swallow-blooded cowards.	
	I'll fetch a tame sheep shall worry you both.	

Sing.

Sight.	Art thou mad? *Simpl.* Art thou not?	
	Search. And thou mad as he.	
Sight.	Am I mad? *Simpl.* Is he mad?	
	Search. Then mad are all three.	630
All.	We all must be mad, 'tis the price of our	
	pain;	
	All mortals are mad, when the mad planets	
	reign.	
Simpl.	But this is nothing.	
Search.	Why shall we fight? *Sight.* How shall we	
	fight?	
Search.	When shall we fight? *Sight.* Where shall we	
	fight?	
Simpl.	Why shall we fight, sayst thou, in the first	
	place?	
Search.	Aye, why?	
Simpl.	Why, for example and for fashion's sake.	
	Do not I tell you? All the	

---

[14] Read *is spoken truly* for *truly*.

75

	shepherds in Arcadia are at it, and for	
	they know not what.	
Search.	Well then, how shall we fight?	
Simpl.	Why, thou shalt beat him, and I will beat	
	thee.	640
Search, Sight.	And who shall beat thee?	
Simpl.	For that, let me alone. Trouble not your-	
	selves. If I find not	
	one to beat me, call me Simplicity again.	
Sight.	Well, when and where shall we fight?	
[Simpl.]	When, but now, and where, but here, etc.	645

Dance, kick and beat each other.

Exit, halting off.[15]

[Time.]	Laugh, laugh, and hold thy sides, old Time,	
	to see thy madness work	
	among 'em. Oh, these are some I look for.	
	It takes the higher powers.	

Enter Fortune and Virtue.

Fortune.	Now gip, goody Virtue. Are you grown so	
	rampant?	
Virtue.	Fie, mistress Fortune. Virtue is above you,	
	though now you have wrought	
	your ends on her, you slight her.	650
Fortune.	What end, I pray, forsooth?	
Virtue.	Thy birth of Honor, proud forgetful dame,	
	Which Juno but for me had ne'er delivered.	
	But I can stop her growth and blast her glories	
	Spite of thy power, if once I forsake her.	655
Fortune.	Alas, poor beggar.	
Virtue.	'Tis not thy wealth can buy a thought of mine,	
	Glorious, inglorious strumpet.	
Time.	[Aside] Virtue scolds.	
Fortune.	Strumpet!	
Virtue.	Thousands there are that daily calls thee	
	whore;	660

15 This stage direction is repeated in the MS.

	The worst they say by me is I am poor.
Fortune.	They are heretics that know not how to use
	A fortune—robbers, gamesters, and the like—
	that so blaspheme my name.
Virtue.	Art thou not cursed by sea and land for
	mutabilities
	In councils, states, and 'specially in wars?

The worst they say by me is I am poor.

Fortune. They are heretics that know not how to use
A fortune—robbers, gamesters, and the like—
that so blaspheme my name.

Virtue. Art thou not cursed by sea and land for
mutabilities
In councils, states, and 'specially in wars? 665

Fortune. Speak lower, Virtue; I can trip you there.
Are not the breaches, blows, and batteries,
Retreats, pursuits, conquests, and victories
Through blood and horror in the fields of war
The works of Virtue oft as much as Fortune? 670
And when great conquerors have been conquered,
has not
The cause been oftentimes for that their virtue
Forsook them, not their fortune?

Virtue. I am of your blind side. They forsook me.
But grant it so. Thousands for one have fallen 675
Whose fortune forsook them before their virtue—
Some in the midst of the race, some at the end,
Which yet are counted happy in this point:
That life and fortune left them at one instant.
Others again have been unfortunate 680
In so long living that you took occasion
To turn your back and make their age inglorious.
Have I not oped a vein now that takes wind?

Fortune. Thy words are nothing else. Go scold among
the beggars, your companions.

Virtue. You may find yours in the brothels or the
hospitals. 685

Exit.

[Time.] Ha, ha. Virtue has got the better on it.

Exit Fortune.[16]

---

[16] The MS. assigns the line and stage direction to Fortune, but the line is
clearly Time's and the exit, Fortune's.

77

Juno.	I may not suffer long this great unrest.
Time.	Who next appears?

Enter Honor and Love.

Honor.	What art thou, malapert boy, that thus pursuest me?	
Love.	You have said, lady—I am a malapert boy.	690
Honor.	What's thy condition or thy quality?	
Love.	I am a liege agent here in Arcadia	
	For the high and mighty Cupid, god of Love.	
Honor.	Art thou not Love himself in a disguise to betray Honor?	
Love.	It was shrewdly guessed. You see, I have no wings nor bow or quiver.	695
	But in my master Love's behalf I claim	
	Precedence of you, my lady Honor.[17]	
	The swains and nymphs all subscribe to me	
	And scorn your supercilious dignity.	
Honor.	Thou, then, shalt be the ruin of them all.	700
Love.	Their creed runs contrary. They only fear	
	That Honor shall destroy them.	
	The mirths, the pleasures, the free sports and pastimes	
	Which I supply them with, they hold their life.	
Honor.	But still I'll read other principles and teach 'em that	705
	Good name, fair name, sweet reputation.[18]	
	Bright honor, and illustrious glory are	
	The five rich treasures of lady, which,	
	If once she lose, her life itself is loathsome.	
Love.	Heresy, heresy. Here's no ground to hear it.	710
	Nor shall Time suffer it.	
Honor.	Then, Honor flee. This country has no dwelling place for me.	

[17] In the MS. *master* reads *m^rs*.
[18] In the MS. *reputation* reads *repution*.

Love.	Not so fast, Honor. You'll infect other countries.
	No, you are a prisoner unto Time. Lock her up.
Time.	Ha, ha, ha. I have a dungeon here that shall
	obscure her 715
	From the world's eye. Down, Honor. Down, down, down.
Honor.	Oh Virtue, Juno, help! Oh, stay; oh, stay!
	[Time] exit with Honor.
Love.	They do not hear you, and I must away.
	Exit.
Juno.	Yes, Juno hears, but for your saucy pranks
	Will in fit time requite you with due thanks. 720
	Enter Time.
Time.	So Honor's fast. My little madcap Love
	has done me service in it and may effect
	more mischief in his madness.
	Would he could bring in Desert to keep her company.
	Enter Age with fancies tied
	in his hair and beard.
	Sing.[19]
Age.	"Turn, Amaryllis, to thy swain,
	Thy Damon calls thee back again." 725
	What a strange burden love is whose flames
	I cannot get
	the means to quench.
Time.	*[Aside]* So, so. Age with his wanton fit upon him.
Age.	Why do the nymphs thus fly me? Seem I not youthful, handsome,
	and well-favored? And am I not as amiably dressed 730
	as other amorites are? This fancy do I wear
	for Amaryllis. This (aye, this) for Cloris.

[19] In the MS. *Sing* appears in the speech tag column before line 724; *Age* appears before line 725.

79

This for sweet Lesbia, and this for Licoris.
Yet they all fly me with their nimbler feet.
My stripling boy, too, when he should assist me   735
To catch and trip their heels up, gets abroad
And leaves me hoarse with holloing after
   them.

Juno.   [*Aside*] How monstrous, how prodigious does
   this appear in Age.

Time.   [*Aside*] Laugh, Time, on thy revenge. Age sleeps
   upon a bed of nettle seeds.

Sing.[20]

Age.   Hoy boy, hoy boy. Come, come away, boy,   740
And bring me my longing desire—
A lass that is neat and can well do the feat,
When lusty young blood is afire.

Let her waist be small, though her body
   be tall,
And her age not above eighteen.   745
Let her care for no bed, but here let her
   spread
Her mantle upon this green.

Let her face be fair and her breast be bare.
A voice, let her have, that can warble.
Let her belly be soft, but to mount me
   aloft,   750
Let her bouncing buttocks be marble.
Hay, come away, boy.

Time.   [*Aside*] Oh brave old boy.

Juno.   [*Aside*] How odious, how preposterous is this
   in Age, but 'tis Time's madness
that infects him.

Enter Desert and Danger.

[20] In the MS. *Sing* appears in the speech tag column before line 740; *Age* appears before line 741.

80

Age.	She comes! And a brave hunting nymph with
	a bow and quiver. [*Aside*] One 755
	of Diana's, I suppose, that's weary of her
	maidenhead.
Time.	[*Aside*] Desert is come within my bounds. Oh,
	that Security were here to
	charm that monster. Then she were mine.
Age.	Well met, sweet marjorum fair. Which way
	go you?
Danger.	Hogh!
Age.	And "hogh" to thee, foot. What are thou
	for? A pimp, major? 760
Desert.	Fly, good old man. My follower will kill
	thee else.
Age.	I fear no followers. I am for the leader and
	dare fight for a wench with Beelzebub.
Desert.	Good Age, forbear. Thou dotest upon thy
	death.
Age.	Who's [it] that tells me of age? Hah! Or
	if I loved, or I dote?
Danger.	Die, dotard, thee. 765
	Enter Security [who] holds
	his club and parts them.
Secur.	Not so, fell monster. Age, be thou secure,
	and live, Desert.
Time.	[*Aside*] Security is come.
Secur.	While I am with you, all is safe and sure.
	Music.
	Pray sit and hear the music that attends me.
Danger.	Yes, I love music.
Age.	And so do I, but not to sit so nigh that
	ugly, devil-faced rascal. 770
	Security sings.
	Danger and Age fall asleep.
	Security takes away Danger's club.

81

Secur.	This goes with me. Time, I have done thee service.
	[Exit Security.]
Time.	Gramercie, sweet Security. Now, lady, you are mine and must with me.
Desert.	Time will not be my enemy, I hope.
Time.	Flatter not yourself.

Honor and you, Desert, are now my prisoners.
Fortune and Virtue, too, I have in chain(s),
in which condition I will starve you all.   775
Exit carrying Desert.

Desert.	Help! Help! Oh, Juno, help!
Time.	Ha, ha, ha.
Juno.	I see and pity thy distress, sweet nymph,

And all the rest that in Arcadia now suffer
    by the lunacy of Time,
Whom I must purge for the recovery
Of Age, of Will, of Judgment, Sight and
    Search,   780
Of Fortune, Virtue, Honor, and Desert,
Of poor Simplicity and Love himself—all
    metamorphosed.
But Danger being taken at advantage,
Disarmed, shall in the first place be removed.
Holla, you rugged satyrs that do haunt   785
Those bushy thickets there, come forth,
Enter Satyrs, 6 or 7.
And with your active horns toss up that
    monster, Danger,
Unto my Clouds, whence I command to carry him
Until they let him fall into the sea.
But first, with tender hands remove old Age   790
And let him sleep secure within that bower
    'til I descend.
They carry in Age.

1st Satyr.	'Tis done, great goddess.

Juno.	Now triumph over Danger in your dances.
	Dance.
	In the dance they trample and
	abuse him; Danger roars.
Juno.	So now away to sea with him and there
	Upon the main only let him appear, 795
	While I to my Arcadia restore
	The peace and happiness she had before.
	Finis Actus Quarti

Act V

Enter Juno and Love.[21]

Juno.	You are well found, sir. Where's your master,
	Age?
Love.	I do not know, indeed. Forsooth, I have here
	a master, now I lost
	him, forsooth, and know not where to find
	him. 800
Juno.	Then I do know. And now, sir, I know you—
	for all your disguise and
	your counterfeit childish language.
Love.	Indeed, Aunt, I am very sick. This Time
	has undone us all.
Juno.	Well, sir, because you have felt some smart
	for your waggery, I'll work
	for your recovery and help you to your arms
	again. 805
Love.	O, heavenly aunt.
Juno.	Ho, Age. Where art thou? Awake. Come forth.
	Enter Age without his toys.
Age.	Your power has waked me, and by your great
	virtue—

---

[21] In the MS. *Love* reads *boue.*

	now that I see your excellence—I find	
	that I have walked in error and in wildness,	810
	forgetting duty to my sovereign goddess.	
Juno.	There was your fault; thence came your	
	punishment.	
Age.	But I was struck by Time into that frenzy.	
Juno.	But Time was first abused and poisoned here	
	with Envy and her brood, which, Age, you are	
	guilty of	815
	by your transgressions and neglect of duty.	
	Do you not know this stripling here?	
Age.	I had a lad like him.	
Juno.	'Tis he. 'Tis wanton Love. I have discovered	
	him.	
Age.	Then there it is. Before I took him in	820
	As a distressed child (oh cruel counterfeit),	
	I lived in solitary hermitage.	
	By wholesome labor for my daily food,	
	To maintain life unto no other end	
	But that my hands might not be void of work,	825
	Nor my heart empty of devotion.	
Juno.	'Twas a good life. You shall be well again.	
	Come and attend me, both. Here, Time,	
	come forth.	

Enter Time bound about the
head and hugely in the belly.

Time.	To obey you, I must.	
Juno.	How now, Time, not well?	830
Time.	No, I'm very sick.	
Juno.	Very much swollen, methinks, too.	
Love.	O huge and monstrous Time.	
Juno.	Come. I'll be your physician. Go, Age; make	
	this medicine instantly.	

Exit Age.

	Time, you are taken into my cure,	835
	And I must purge you, Time, of those foul evils	

84

	That are within you ere I can restore	
	Those that by you are driven into distractions,	
	As Fortune, Virtue, Judgment, Will, and others,	
	Desert, Honor, which you keep in prison.	840
Time.	Fortune and Virtue, too. I have them fast.	
Juno.	Will you release 'em now?	
Time.	I'll release none.	
Juno.	Are you so cross? I shall cross you anon.	
Love.	Cross him not, Madam. Time is splayfooted.	845
	Nor stand so near. He has an unsavory breath.	
	His belching stomach's full of barking libels.	
[Juno.]	'Tis but the crabbedness of his disease.	
	We'll see anon what stuff he's full [of], withal.	

Enter Age with a vial.

	Come, Age, let's see. Have you composed it well?	850
Time.	What's that you'll give me?	
Juno.	A composition made of the extractions	
	Of several herbs that grow here in Arcadia.	
	The chiefest of them is the herb of grace,	
	Bitter in taste but sweet in operation. It shall work gently with you.	855
Time.	You tell me gently, but I fear the soothings of the physician.	
Juno.	Would you have your health? Take him in, Age. Give it him and keep him near.	

Exit Age, Time.[22]

	[Love.] Juno's the doctor; Age, the apothecary; and I, the apothecary's man.	
	If Time were to be glistered, now that were my office.	
	I would so play upon his breech-work.	860

Time. *Within.*[23] Oh! Oh! Oh! Oh!

---

[22] This stage direction follows line 856 in the MS.
[23] In the MS. *Within* appears slightly above the speech tag *Time.*

85

Love.	He has taken it. It troubles his foul stomach.
Time.	Oh! Oh! Oh! Oh!
Love.	Faugh! Faugh! It works already. O, all Arcadia, stop your noses. Time's sickness leaves a stinking farewell for you. See. Here's one of his diseases vomited already.

Enter Envy.

	'Tis Envy. I know the hag.	
Juno.	Away with her!	865
Love.	Out of this kingdom, whore. To hell! To hell!	
Envy.	I am gone. I am gone.	

Exit; kick her out.

Love.	Hold his head hard, Age, that he may fetch all up.

Enter Suspicion, Jealousy.

	See? Here's Suspicion; here's false Jealousy. Away, you mischiefs. Fly and follow your leader to the devil!	870

Exit.

Time.	Oh! Oh! Oh! Oh!	
Love.	There's more to come yet, it seems.	
Time.	Oh! Oh! Oh! Oh! Oh! ——Oh! Oh! ——Oh! Oh!	
Love.	Now, now up it comes and down it goes. What a damnable bellyful had this Time. Would it were all out yet. So, so, so. There's Malice, Hatred, and Revenge.	875

Enter Malice, Hatred, Revenge.

On in the name to Pluto, down to Erebus.

Exeunt.

86

See, see? For as many mischiefs as come
    upwards and out,
there's thrice the number gone downwards and
    out by the
backside. You may give me leave to lie a
    little. I should not
talk like a 'pothecary else. Now he breaks
    wind like a tempest,   880
and all that comes from him is swearing
    oaths and lies of all kinds
and colors. He farts diurnals and weekly
    intelligences. How devilishly
was this Time popped up and peppered to have
    all those in his belly
at once. What a timpani was there. But here
    he comes now, recovered
and as gaunt as ever he was since his nonage.
    Now   885
I speak within compass.

               Enter Time and Age.

Juno.	How is it with you now, Time?
Time.	Thanks, gracious Juno, perfectly well.
	Methinks I am young again.
Juno.	Beware of such excess hereafter, Time.
Age.	I am perfect Age again, thanks to your grace. 890
Love.	And Love is well-amended. Time's recovery
	will cure all, I hope.
[Juno.]	Now, Time, release your prisoners and restore
	All those that run abroad beside themselves.
[Time.]	All shall be done to Juno's divine will.
	And here come some of them. First, Sight
	grown purblind, 895
	and Search in a dead palsy; Will lame on
	crutches;
	Judgment turned idiot; Simplicity, a roarer.

Enter Sight, Search,
Will, Judgment, Simplicity.
They all show action accordingly.

Juno.   Alas, poor hearts. How they are all trans-
            formed.

[Time.]   Now by your power I will restore them to their
            conditions. 'Tis done.
            I'll now enlarge my prisoners.   900
                                        Exit.

Judg.   Thanks, divine Juno. We are now ourselves.

Sight.   I can now see again o'er all the world,
            and hope to see fair dealing in it again.

Search.   And I can search as nimbly as a mouse or a
            hired constable at midnight.

Simpl.   And for my part, I will now go a fishing
            again, for truly, in   905
            my simple judgment, Simplicity is safer at
            sea than on the
            land. I'll be no more a swordfish ashore.

Will.   My will is now become the same it was,
            The servant of Desert. But she is lost.
            The worst effect of Time's apostasy   910
            Has been the parting of that nymph and me.

Juno.   She is your mistress, then.

Will.   My soul waits on her.

Judg.   Will, let my sorrows give thy heart some ease.
            Thou sufferest not alone. The sun by setting
            ne'er made the world more sad and silent than
            Virtue's departure   915
            has made me.

[Juno.]   Is she your mistress, Judgment?

Judg.   The soul of my affection.

Age.   But where is Honor? There's the noblest
            nymph.

Juno.   Age, dost thou love her?

Age.	She is the crown of age set with a thousand
	amiable looks 920
	More precious than diamonds. She wears
	A thousand comely graces in her carriage
	And her discourses are, though she be young,
	Restorative instructions for old age.
Love.	I honor Fortune most. 925
Juno.	Dost thou, Cupid? Why?
Love.	Since Desert got my arms and my mother my
	wings, I have played
	at hazard and dealt no certainty. Therefore,
	if I make
	a blind match with her, I may live upon
	uncertainty.
Juno.	'Tis very well considered. 930

Enter Time, Fortune,
Virtue, Honor, Desert.

	See, the four nymphs in question.
Will.	Am I so blest to see Desert again?
Love.	And Fortune, if you will have a finger for
	Love, Love will have a hand for you.
Fortune, Virtue, Honor.	Love?
Juno.	'Tis even he.
Sight.	What a brave interview is this! 935
Search.	We shall have matches and marriages, feasts,
	if I search well into this
	matter.
Simpl.	Truly, for my part and in my simple judgment,
	it is a joyful
	sight to see. I never saw a better unless
	'twere once my net
	full of salmons at a draught. 940
Juno.	Now, my fair nymphs, how do you find
	yourselves?
Virtue.	Well, thanks, Juno. But we have been very
	ill-handled by Time.

89

Time.	Time now repents of all the ill he did.
Juno.	After your close restraint now, if you had
	each one a husband,
	would it not appear a double freedom? 945
Fortune.	Perhaps a stricter bondage.
Juno.	Perhaps, indeed, in that you speak yourself,
	Fortune, but when
	true love joins and remains, marriage is
	ever freedom and no bondage.
Will.	Great goddess, all the shepherds honor you,
	And Will above the rest has vowed to serve you 950
	For favor shown unto his nymph, Desert.
Juno.	Will, thou are worthy who hast made Desert
	The only object of thy love and actions.
Desert.	'Tis he, indeed, who in election
	Hath preferred me before all other nymphs. 955
Juno.	Take her and cherish her. And, as she is
	Desert, she will advance thee.
Love.	Mistress Desert, I hope you need not these
	for an addition to your portion.
Desert.	Sweet Love, resume thine arms. Use them
	thyself
	Now, since my Will and I are knit together.
Love.	[*Aside*] Now, Love, thou art a deity again, 960
	And have at Honor presently for my old master
	To gratify his love to me. No, I'll not
	shoot,
	But win her fairly of her mother. [*To Fortune*]
	Fortune.
Fortune.	What is your will, Cupid?
Love.	Honor, you know, is full of hot blood, and
	Age is cold tempered. Her 965
	heat with his cold, and his cold with her
	heat and they shall both
	so cure and compose each other that there

90

	can be no such match	
	in all the world.	

Take Fortune and Honor aside.

Sight.	Sure Love is blind to match her to Age. Does	
	he not see how he sheds his teeth?	970
Simpl.	Truly by that he should be young again, for	
	children do so.	
Search.	I would never match her with a porter. He	
	grows cracked with his burden.	
Sight.	Burden? What burden?	
Search.	He carries a hundred years upon his back.	
	What thinkst thou, Simplicity?	
Simpl.	Truly, for my part and in my simple judg-	
	ment, a young man	975
	were fitter for her, for if a lover be not	
	like a fish—ever new—he's naught.	
Search.	Well said, fisherman.	
Honor.	I hear your vulgar censure and despise 'em.	
	Youth is 'cumbered with a world of follies,	
	And Honor overthrows a fool. Give me to Age.	980
Fortune.	Age, there be many motions in thee that	
	procure	
	My full consent. Here, take her for an	
	ornament	
	To thee. Be thou a guide to her.	
Juno.	Virtue, here's Judgment with a steadfast eye	
	Fastened upon you, courts you with his	
	thoughts.	985
Judg.	Since my first sight of her, my thoughts	
	have ever	
	Preserved me her true servant.	
[Virtue.]	Virtue by Judgment ever was promoted,	
	And he ——— I will live with thee.[24]	

24 Unreadable word or words in the MS.

91

Juno.	Fortune, you see Love has his arms restored, 990
	All but his flyers. If you and he were
	matched
	And the sick feathers taken out of your wings,
	And then your wings were fastened unto him,
	All the whole kingdom here of Love were
	happy.
Fortune.	To gratify Juno, Fortune is content. 995
Simpl.	So, so. Cupid has taken Fortune without hook
	or bait.
[Love.]	Kiss me, gallant Fortune, and fasten thy wings
	unto me. If there
	be no fault in thy feathers, Love shall never
	be inconstant.[25]
Juno.	Each take his own by the hand and let us move 1000
	To tread out mischief and replant true love.

Dance.

[Shout within.][26]

	Hark how by secret inspirations
	Arcadia, released from her distractions,
	In triumph shouts for joy of those great
	matches—
	Desert with Will, Virtue with Judgment met, 1005
	Honor to Age, and Love to Fortune set.
	These are strong bonds after a sad decrease
	For a confirmation of a future peace.
All.	Thanks to great Juno.

Finis

Deus his dedit quoque finem

[25] Line 999 is struck out in the MS.

[26] In the MS. *Shout within* appears at line 997 where the speech tag *Love* has been added.

Explanatory Notes

Nomina Actorum: The swains, nymphs, Security, and some of Envy's hags, who appear in the play, are not listed here. The omissions may be because they are doubled roles. See the Introduction, p. 38.

3. present: immediate, actually at hand.

5. Cf. "Oh, 'tis the Paradise, the Heaven of earth" (Chapman, *All Fools*, 1.1.3); "this earthly paradise of wedlock" (*All Fools*, 3.1.245). The playwright may also have had in mind Shakespeare's lines:

> This other Eden, demi-paradise,
> This fortress built by Nature for herself
> Against infection and the hand of war,
> This happy breed of men, this little world,
> This precious stone set in the silver sea,
> Which serves it in the office of a wall
> Or as a moat defensive to a house,
> Against the envy of less happier lands,
> This blessed plot, this earth, this realm,
>   this England.
>   [*Richard II*, 2.1.42–51]

6. Arcadia: In classical geography, Arcadia was a mountainous district in the center of the Peloponnesus. Its idealization as a region of rustic contentment by Virgil (*Eclogues* 4, 7, 10) and others has some factual basis. Mainly a rural community of hill pastures and hunting grounds, Arcadia was the original home of the worship of Pan, the shepherd's god, and it remained the chief center of his cult and of the pastoral music which he purportedly invented and patronized. The Arcadian literature of the Renais-

93

sance, influenced by the Arcadia of the Italian writer Sannazzaro, includes the pastorals of Sidney, Spenser, Greene, and others. Milton's *Arcades*, a brief masque, was written about 1633, and Shirley's play *Arcadia* (a dramatization of Sidney's poem) was first performed in 1640.

7. intellect: "wits" or "sense." Very common in the seventeenth and eighteenth centuries (*OED*).

10. This river image recurs in the play. See lines 341–342, 493, 576–577.

12. rapine: A possible reference to the Parliamentary army's desecration of churches.

15. alchemy: chemistry.

19–26. This relationship between Sight and Search and their masters remains undeveloped in the play. See the Introduction, p. 25.

28. entire: "complete"; also "sincere, genuine" (*OED*); proverbial, "The things of friends are in common" (*The Oxford Dictionary of English Proverbs*, comp. William George Smith [Oxford: Oxford University Press, 1936]).

32–33. Note that nothing is said about Will's having followed Virtue; it is not in the nature of Will to do so.

34–35. See line 368. Otherwise, not much is made of Envy as a follower of Virtue. Spenser says that Envy hates good works and virtuous deeds (*FQ*, 5.12.32). In *The Magnificent Entertainment* devised by Thomas Dekker, Envy "rages" against the Four Stoic Virtues and against King James's four kingdoms, "for very madness . . . feeding on the heads of adders" (*The Dramatic Works of Thomas Dekker*, ed. R. H. Shepherd, I, 318). For other analogues, see the Introduction, pp. 43–44.

42–50. For the manner of Juno's entrance, which alludes to discovery scenes in masques and plays, see the Introduction, pp. 35–36, and for possible sources, see p. 44.

57. Cf. "This in the region of the air shall stand" (Chapman, "Ovid's Banquet," *The Poems of George Chapman*, ed. Phyllis Brooks Bartlett, p. 30, noted by J. D. Jump, "The Anonymous

Masque in MS. Egerton 1994," *Review of English Studies* 2 [April, 1935]: 190).

80ff. Contention between Fortune and Virtue is a frequent emblem in medieval and Renaissance moral philosophy. An early and extremely influential account of their relationship is in Boethius's *The Consolation of Philosophy.* The alliance of Fortune and Virtue often figures in entertainments designed as tributes to royalty; the two figure, for example, in the triumphal arch designed by Thomas Dekker for the reception of King James (Dekker, *Complete Works,* I, 317–318). Also see Samuel C. Chew, *The Pilgrimage of Life,* p. 68.

86–89. The blackthorn (sloe) often blooms in late winter. Cf. "Like to the hatching of the blackthorn's spring, / With bitter frosts, and smarting hailstorms, forth" (Chapman, *Poems,* p. 250, noted by Jump, "The Anonymous Masque," p. 190).

93–95. frame: an established order, plan, scheme, esp. of government (*OED*). For analogues, see the Introduction, p. 43.

96. In Jonson's *Cynthia's Revels,* Virtue is "a poor Nymph . . . that's scarce able to buy herselfe a gowne . . ." (*The Works of Ben Jonson,* ed. C. H. Herford and Percy Simpson, IV, Induction, lines 89ff.).

106. Time later starves the virtues in Arcadia. See line 775.

109ff. A similar idea is expressed in Thomas Carew's *Coelum Britannicum* (1634) when Fortune says, "I gave the dignity, but you made the vice."

115–116. unnatural strife: A probable reference to the Civil War. See the Introduction, pp. 7–8. Cf. John Taylor, "An humble DESIRED UNION between PREROGATIVE and Privilege . . ." (1642), who compares his time with "the unnatural dissension that bloodily embrewed this Kingdom 80 and od yeares betwixt the Royal Families of *Yorke* and *Lancaster* . . ." (*The Works of John Taylor*).

125. Lucina: goddess of parturition. See the Introduction, p. 21.

128–129. Fortune "is painted also with a wheel, to signify to you, which is the moral of it, that she is turning and inconstant, and mutability, and variation . . ." (*Henry V*, 3.4.26ff.). Fortune carries her wheel in Robert White's *Cupid's Banishment* and in Carew's *Coelum Britannicum*. In Chapman's *Masque of the Middle Temple and Lincoln's Inn*, her wings are "likewise hung in a conspicuous place, and there is described 'that rich Temple, where Fortune fixed those her golden wings, thou seest, and that rolling stone she used to tread upon for sign she never would forsake this kingdom' " (11.163–165, quoted in Jump, "The Anonymous Masque," pp. 188–189).

133. Time's wings: In Renaissance and Baroque art, Father Time is generally winged. See Erwin Panofsky, *Studies in Iconology*, p. 71. The character Time who appears in act 3 is not winged, however.

136. soft measure: "Measure" here probably does not refer to the grave and stately measures danced at the courts of Elizabeth I and James I, for the term had come by this time to signify a dance generally. "Soft" suggests a *basse danse*, possibly the pavane, which was popular from 1530 to about 1676. The pavane was not much more than formal, patterned walking to a slow tempo, often accompanied by the hautboy. See Louis Horst, *Pre-Classic Dance Forms*, pp. 7–20. Also see the note to line 556.

137. See the Introduction, p. 44.

141–144. I have been unable to locate this allusion. It is possible that the playwright made it up. Scarabs, or dung beetles, collect the dung of animals, shape it into a ball, lay their eggs in it, and then bury it. The dunghill scarabs anticipate the purgation of Time in act 5, and Jupiter protects the Eagle's eggs as Juno protects Fortune's Honor and the fruitfulness of all Arcadia. The contrast in the allusion between birth and feces is recurrent in the play.

155–156. soldiers: The lack of facilities for treating and supporting wounded soldiers was a matter of great concern in the 1640's, particularly after the outbreak of the Civil War. John Evelyn finds remarkable Holland's "Hospital for their lame and decrepid soldiers" (*The Diary of John Evelyn*, ed. E. S. de Beer,

96

II, 45–46). After the outbreak of the war, the problems of poverty and unemployment were increased because of returning wounded soldiers. Beginning in 1642 a series of ordinances was passed, the first stating that Parliament would provide adequately for those wounded in its service. Six months later, however, it was clear that Parliament could not take care of the problem, and an ordinance of March, 1643, states that "that course cannot be held for any continuance of time without many inconveniences." Responsibility for the soldiers was shifted to their parishes, which proved to be an equally ineffective solution. Both sides were notorious for not paying their armies. See Margaret James, *Social Problems and Policy During the Puritan Revolution, 1640–1660*, pp. 243, 254ff.

158–160. Cf. John Taylor, "The Papist, and the Schismatique: both grieves / The *Church*, for shee's like *Christ* (Between two thieves)" ("Mad Fashions, od fashions . . . ," *Works of John Taylor*). Since the 1630's Puritans had been buying tithes which had fallen into the hands of laymen in order to subsidize nonconformist lecturers. After the outbreak of the war, about one-fourth of the high church and loyalist clergy were evicted from their parishes. Determined to rid churches of popish ceremonies and to destroy all marks of "superstition," the parliamentary armies often drove away their clergymen as well. See Arnold Tindal Hart, *The Country Clergy in Elizabethan and Stuart Times, 1558–1660*, pp. 112ff., and H. O. Wakeman, *The Church and the Puritans, 1570–1660*, pp. 140ff.

161–162. Many of the leading members of the Commons were lawyers who used their knowledge of the law to "search for causes" to justify those actions which Parliament took as they began to intrude on royal prerogative. Manipulation of the law by parliamentary lawyers was a matter of much discussion in the early years of the Civil War. See James, *Social Problems and Policy*, pp. 326ff., and John William Allen, *English Political Thought*, pp. 302ff.

s.d. 164–165. Simplicity: The character of Simplicity, the fisherman, introduces a touch of the piscatory eclogue. In his seven

Piscatory Eclogues (1633) Phineas Fletcher follows Sannazzaro in substituting fishermen for shepherds, as he also did in his play *Sicelides*, acted at King's College, Cambridge, and printed in 1631. A Simplicity appears in Jonson's *Cynthia's Revels*. See the Introduction, p. 44.

172. damoisel of France: Probably a reference to Charles I's queen, Henrietta Maria of France, whose love of dancing and court entertainments was famous (or, according to Prynn, infamous).

179. the gods make quick work, you know: In Greek and Roman mythology many gods and goddesses are born full-grown.

182. My heart gave me: "my heart tells (or suggests) to me" (*OED*).

184. That is, scrambling for Fortune's treasure. Perhaps an allusion to the proverb "He that hath little shall have less" (John Clarke, *Paroemiologia Anglo-Latina in Usum Scholarum Concinnata*, p. 82).

188. pun on porpoise: porpisce, "poor fish."

194. Neptune: in classical mythology, the god of the sea, usually represented as bearded, with the trident as his chief attribute. Pisces: the twelfth sign of the zodiac, the fishes. Aquarius: the eleventh sign of the zodiac, the water-bearer.

196. Pun on love, Cupid, passion.

199–200. Sight is referring to some of Cupid's best-known qualities. Usually depicted as a cherub, he wields tremendous power, hence the oxymoron. "Weight" probably alludes to the heaviness of the passion which he inflicts with his arrows. A familiar iconographic motif is that of Cupid with a weight attached to one wrist and wings to another, which can suggest either love's being hindered by the present life or the soaring and sinking emotions of the lover. His heat is alluded to by Jonson in the *Haddington Masque* (*Works of Ben Jonson*, VII): "All his bodie is a fire / All his breath a flame entire."

202. According to Hesiod, Venus sprang from the foam of the sea that gathered about the severed penis of Uranus when Cronos

mutilated him. Botticelli's *The Birth of Venus* is a familiar Renaissance interpretation of this story. For the association between Love and Venus in the play, see the Introduction, p. 24.

208. Often personified in Renaissance literature, Desert may be male or female. In George Wither's eclogue *The Shepherd's Hunting* there is a refernce to "a nymph that hight Desart" (George Wither, *Juvenalia*, I, 97). For the relationship between Love, Desert, and Danger, see the Introduction, p. 43.

210. Cupid, Love: Cupid's name changes at this point and remains Love for the rest of the play; the two names were often synonymous. The author may have picked up the speech tag "Cupid" from following Chapman. See the Introduction, pp. 40ff., and the Appendix.

215–252. For the connection between these lines and the masque scene in George Chapman's *Byron's Tragedy*, see the Introduction, pp. 39–43. Chapman's masque is reprinted as the Appendix.

222. golden fetters: "Golden," an addition to Chapman's line, may be a recollection of Spenser's

> And wrapt in fetters of a golden tress
> That can with melting pleasaunce mollify
> Their hardened hearts, enur'd to blood and
> cruelty.
>
> [*FQ*, 5.8.1]

The more usual form of the proverb is "No man loveth his fetters, be they made of gold."

225. ravished: "transported, entranced, enraptured" (*OED*).

227. relish: This musical ornament consists in the more or less rapid alternation of the main note with a tone or semitone above it. Patterns for a relish varied, some becoming very complex, but basically a relish is similar to a trill (Sir George Grove [ed.], *Dictionary of Music and Musicians*, 5th ed. [New York: St. Martin's Press, 1954]).

228. ran division: The heart of Renaissance musical embellishment lay in the notion of division: quite literally, it is the divid-

ing up (or breaking down) of long notes into figures compounded of shorter connecting notes (Grove, *Dictionary of Music and Musicians*). Cf. "He could not run division with more art upon his quaking instrument" (John Ford, *Lover's Melancholy*, in *The Works of John Ford*, ed. William Gifford and Alexander Dyce, I: 1.1.14).

235–236. Venus and Adonis: This allusion, which does not appear in Chapman's masque, refers to the death of Adonis, killed by a boar while hunting. Venus, who loved him, caused the rose or anemone to spring from his blood. The story of the love of Venus for Adonis, one of the most popular of the Renaissance, comes from Book X of Ovid's *Metamorphoses*.

238. shepherd's shape: Love's costume provides a way to avoid the iconographic demands for nakedness.

247. hazard: a frequent pun in the Renaissance. *Hazard* is both a dicing game and a tennis term. Openings in the inner wall of the tennis court were called hazards. See line 927. Cf. "I have set my life upon a cast, / And I will stand the Hazard of the die" (*Richard III*, 5.4.9).

252. headed: (1) to direct the course of, (2) to fit with an arrowhead, (3) to be at the head of.

256. Venus's renunciation of Love: Burton tells one story of Cupid's banishment from heaven and another of Venus's threating to break his bows and arrows and to clip his wings (Robert Burton, *The Anatomy of Melancholy*, III, 42).

261. mischief: as "a cause or source of harm or evil," the word had a much stronger connotation in the seventeenth century than it has now (*OED*). See lines 387, 870.

264–265. Cf. Cupid: "By Venus' apron-strings, Bacchus, methinks I am nobody now I am disarm'd . . ." (Robert White, *Masque of Cupid's Banishment*, in John Nichols, *Progresses of James I*, III, 290).

270. Love and Fortune's feathers: see note to lines 128–129. In Robert White's *Masque of Cupid's Banishment*, Fortune wears "a rich mantle wrought with changeable colours to express her un-

certainty." Love's comment is slightly ironic, since he is also often depicted as changeable, sometimes, for example, by his holding a chameleon.

283–286. The verse form suggests that this is a song, although it is not so designated in the stage directions. I have been unable to locate it.

s.d. 287–288. The dance is no doubt a ring dance (a round), one of the elemental forms of group dance, often danced around a central pillar (the maypole, for example) or an honored person. John Playford's *The English Dancing Master* contains music and figures for thirteen rounds to be danced by six, eight, or "as many as will." This country dance contrasts with the more courtly dances in acts 1 and 3. In *Cupid's Banishment* a group of threatening nymphs dances around Cupid.

288–291. It is customary for this writer to rhyme lines important to shifts in mood. See lines 306–307, 719–720, 794–797, for example.

293. Cf. "In all the peace and safety it enjoys" (Chapman's *Byron's Conspiracy*, 3.2.50, noted by Jump, "The Anonymous Masque," p. 190).

s.d. 293–294. Danger: For possible sources of this figure, see the Introduction, p. 43. Spenser's second Danger, described in *The Faerie Queene* (3.12.11), furnishes some of the attributes which Jonson's female Danger, Peira, has in his *Coronation* (lines 499–503); the latter, like this Danger, carries a club.

300. Proverbial: "The longer you look at it, the less you will like it" (*Oxford Dictionary of English Proverbs*, p. 471).

317–318. a commonplace idea; cf. "Virtue may be assail'd but never hurt" (Milton, *Comus*). Desert is also armed with the emblems of Love.

324. list: "please, choose, like." The word was old-fashioned by Shakespeare's day (*OED*).

Act 3, s.d. Time: a frequently personified figure in the Renaissance. See the Introduction, p. 22.

339. Cf. "Happy and blest be Irus" (Chapman's *The Blind Beg-*

gar of Alexandria, l. 72, noted by Jump, "The Anonymous Masque," p. 190).

341. Cf. "in such a flourishing peace" (Chapman's *Byron's Tragedy*, 4.2.235, noted by Jump, "The Anonymous Masque," p. 190).

347. Security: See lines 357–358. In the Renaissance, Security often implies overconfidence, presumption, carelessness. Cf. "And you all know security / Is mortal's chiefest enemy" (*Macbeth*, 3.5.32–33).

351–353. Time's falling asleep here suggests Sloth, who is almost always shown as being fast asleep.

354. Cf. "soft sleep" (Chapman's "The Shadow of Night," *Poems*, p. 4ª, noted by Jump, "The Anonymous Masque," p. 190).

s.d. 354–355. The playwright gives no clues about this song. The following song, however, survives in four contemporary manuscripts and would be an appropriate choice:

> Care charminage sleepe yᵉ easer of all woes
> Brother of Death sweetly yⁱᵉ selfe disclose
> On this afflicted wight fall like a cloud
> In gentle showers giue nothing yᵗ is loud
> Or painfull to his slumbers but easy sweet
> & as a purling streame yᵘ sone of night pass by
> his
> Troubled senses sing his paine
> Like hollow murmuring winds or silver raine
> Into thy selfe gently o gently o gently slide
> & kiss him into slumbers like a Bride.

For the music and variants of the text, see John P. Cutts, *La Musique de Scène de la Troupe de Shakespeare*, pp. 354ff.

s.d. 354–355. Although these vices are a departure from the traditional seven deadly sins, they are familiar Renaissance abstractions. For possible sources and analogues of the figure of Envy, see the Introduction, pp. 43–44. Suspicion, Malice, and Mischief (or Ate) all appear in Jonson's *Masque of Queens*, and Fear and Jealousy in his *Chloridia* (*Works of Ben Jonson*, VII).

357. "to wax" is to become or turn, sometimes used with reference to a sudden or immediate change (*OED*).

359. fit: "The term *fit* occurs frequently in old copies of drama or ballads . . . indicating an outburst of action and was sometimes applied to a dance form" (Walter George Raffé [ed.], *The Dictionary of the Dance* [New York: A. S. Barnes, 1965]). *Fit* is not listed in the *OED* as an intransitive verb, but a word may have been dropped in the MS.

361–365. Spenser's Suspect is also fearful:

> His rolling eyes did never rest in place
> But walkt each where, for fear of his mischaunce,
> Holding a lattice still before his eyes,
> Through which he still did peepe, as forward
>   he did pace.   [*FQ*, 3.12.15]

382–393. The witches in *Macbeth* also use rhyme for a charm effect.

389. This dance may parody the ring dance in act 2. See the Introduction, p. 31.

s.d. 412–413. See the Introduction, p. 37.

420–422. A familiar emblem, originating in Plato's *Phaedrus*, shows Reason holding a restraining bridle. The image recurs in the play in lines 497 and 532–533.

424. Proverbial: "Time trieth all things" (Clarke, *Paroemiolo gia*, p. 308). Cf. "I Time, that please some, try all . . . (*The Winter's Tale*, 4.1).

433. Cf. Bacon's "Of Envy": "the Act of Envy, has somewhat in it, of Witchcraft. . . ."

435–436. Because Time reveals truth, a common emblem. Proverbial: "Keep counsell first thy selfe" (Clarke, *Paroemiologia*, p. 67).

441. blast: "a sudden infection . . . attributed to the blowing or breath of some malignant power, foul air, etc." (*OED*). See also line 654.

452. Age's blindness: Age's spiritual relapse, suggested by his temporary blindness, will be restored by the "sight" of Juno, Virtue, Fortune, and Honor at line 486.

458–466. Age's desire for a looking glass indicates Pride and

103

Lechery. Although both are frequently shown holding mirrors in medieval and Renaissance iconography, Lechery is usually a female figure.

462–463. Cf. "Love is like a false glass, which represents everything fairer than it is" (Robert Burton, *The Anatomy of Melancholy*, III, 461).

474. to do: *double entendre*; in other words, to have sexual intercourse. Cf. "Look, what you do, you do it still in th' dark" (*Love's Labours Lost*, 5.2.24).

477. Proverbial: "Old men and far travelers may lie by authority" (Clarke, *Paroemiologia*, p. 316).

477–479. A series of bawdy puns: country—cunt; glib bit—(1) slippery bit of food, (2) whore; go down—lie down.

484. knickknacks: trifles. Cf. "You must forget these knickknacks: / A woman, at some time of year, I grant ye / She is necessary; but make no business of her" (Fletcher, *The Humorous Lieutenant*, 1.1.345–347, in *The Works of Francis Beaumont and John Fletcher*, ed. Arnold Glover and A. R. Waller, II).

498. tram: a cunning contrivance or device; a machination, plot, scheme (*OED*).

507. Juno is Cupid's aunt only by the Venus born of Zeus-Jupiter and Dione-Juno. See the Introduction, p. 24, n. 36.

516–517. Juno scolds Jupiter for his various amorous encounters throughout Ovid's *Metamorphoses*.

522–523. housewife: that is, hussy; jilt; light, false woman. Cf. "Let me speak; and let me rail so high / That the false housewife Fortune break her wheel, / Provok'd by my offence" (*Antony and Cleopatra*, 4.15.43–45).

524–525. pun on good/goods. Virtue is poorly dressed.

534–535. Love's lines reflect the fashions of the 1630's and 1640's. Embroidered and perfumed gloves were often given as presents. They were worn, carried, or tucked into the belt. Scarves and elaborate neck chains were worn for display, as were garters —small sashes tied in a large bow below the outer side of the knees. Elegant garters were made of silk, taffeta, cypress, ribbon

104

and net, or cloth of silver or gold and were often fringed with gold or gold braid and trimmed with spantles; usually they cost more than a pound a pair. Unti the 1670's and 1680's ribbon trimming or "fancies" were very popular among the fashionable. See C. Willett Cunnington and Phillis Cunnington, *Handbook of English Costume in the Seventeenth Century*, pp. 49–78.

537–540. Extreme decolletage exposing the breasts was a fashion for unmarried women between 1605 and 1650. "Eye those rising mounts, your displayed breasts, with what shameless art they wooe the shamefast passenger" (R. Braithwait, *The English Gentleman and the English Gentlewoman* [1641], quoted from Phillis Cunnington, *Costume in Pictures*, p. 66).

544–547. "Ladies of Royalist inclination wore their hair in a long thick mass of curls, covering their shoulders and adorned with numerous bows of ribbon." The new fashion of longer hair was partially a reaction to the Puritan women's custom of covering their hair with a cap (1640–1650). Iris Brooke, *English Costume of the Seventeenth Century*, p. 48.

556. measure: See the note to line 136. This dance may be a galliard, which was danced with many kicks, hops, and jumps. In it, everyone danced alone, which may be why Time's presence is not immediately noticed. See Horst, *Pre Classic Dance Forms*, pp. 23–30.

558. Although not all of them did, many Puritans disapproved of dancing. For Honor's association with Puritanism, see the Introduction, p. 25.

574 The song referred to is a ballad by Thomas Deloney. The music composed for it extended its popularity, which was in full force in the reign of James I and continued long after. The words are included in the thirtieth edition of *The Garland of Delight*, by Thomas Deloney, 1681, and in *The Royal Garden of Love and Delight*, edition of 1674. A paraphrase of line 6 appears in Rowley, Dekker and Ford's *The Witch of Edmonton* (performed 1621), 3.1 ("Tarry and kiss me; Sweet Nymph stay"). Four verses are reprinted in *The Roxburghe Ballads* II, 530, and the music is

in William Chappell, *Popular Music of the Olden Time*, I, 338–339. The following is the first verse, which contains the refrain sung by Age:

> When Daphne from faire Phoebus did flie,
>   The west winde most sweetly did blow in her
>   face:
> Her silken scarfe scarce shadowed her eyes;
>   The god cried, "O pitie," and held her in
>   chace.
> "Stay, nymph, stay nymph," cryes Apollo,
>   "Tarry and turn thee; sweet nymph, stay!
> Lion nor tyger doth thee follow;
>   Turn thy faire eyes, and looke this way.
>   O turne, O prettie sweet,
>   And let our red lips meet:
>   Pittie, O Daphne, pittie, O pitty me:
>   Pittie, O Daphne, pittie me."

581. Cf. "Thus the whirligig of time brings in his revenges" (*Twelfth Night*, 5.1.388).

587. together by the ears: quarreling; see also line 619. Proverbial: "A golden apple sets all together by the ears" (Burton, in *Oxford Dictionary of English Proverbs*).

602. hare finding: pun for (1) finding of obliging wenches (hare); (2) pubic hair; (3) the popular sport of hare hunting. See Eric Partridge, *Shakespeare's Bawdy: A Literary and Psychological Essay and a Comprehensive Glossary* (New York: E. P. Dutton & Co., Dutton paperback, 1960).

603. gold finding: alludes to the frequent use of "gold" as a euphemism for feces. Gold finding is privy cleaning. Act 2, scene 1, of Shirley's play *Arcadia* is built on a pun on gold finding. Jakes farmer: privy cleaner.

605. setting for sergeants: a setter was a spy, an informant for police ("sergeants"). From ca. 1630. Eric Partridge, *A Dictionary of Slang and Unconventional English* (New York: The Macmillan Company, 1967).

607. intelligences: spying.

609–611. That is, by looking into the perspective glass (telescope), you will appear as close as if you were right in the bedroom of the courtesan. "Trick" is sexual intercourse; "strike thee blind" refers to one manifestation of the late stages of syphilis.

612–613. constable: the lowest man on the civil service ladder. "You are thought here to be the most senseless and fit man for the constable of the watch" (*Much Ado*, 3.3.23).

615. hen-hearted: timorous. Partridge, *Dictionary of Slang.*

616. roaringest boy: roarer—a riotously noisy reveller or bully: late sixteenth- to early eighteenth-century colloquial. Partridge, *Dictionary of Slang.* See S. Rowland's *A Roaring Boy* (1621) and *A Roaring Boy's Description* (1620).

618. For the political allusions in this scene, see pp. 26–28 of the Introduction. See also lines 637–638.

619. tar box: a box formerly used by shepherds to hold tar as a salve for sheep (*OED*).

620. a word and a blow: proverbial: "Make it a word and a blow" (*Romeo and Juliet*, 3.1.44).

629–632. I have not been able to locate this song. It is probably original.

632. The influence of the seven planets on human character and destiny was a favorite subject of Renaissance art and literature. Cf. "There's some ill planet reigns: / I must be patient till the heavens look / With an aspect more favourable" (*The Winter's Tale*, 2.1.104).

637. for fashion's sake: proverbial; cf. "but yet, for fashion's sake, I thank you too for your society" (*As You Like It*, 3.2.271).

638. gip, goody Virtue: gip: "An exclamation of anger or remonstrance addressed to a horse; an expression of surprise derision, or contempt addressed to a person; = 'get out,' 'go along with you'" (*OED*). Goody: a term of civility formerly applied to a woman, usually a married woman, in humble life (*OED*). For Fortune to call Virtue "goody" is, of course, an insult.

658. strumpet: a frequent epithet of Fortune. Cf. "Out, out thou strumpet, Fortune," (*Hamlet*, 2.2.515).

667. Cf. "Blowes, batteries, breaches" (Chapman's *Byron's Tragedy*, 3.1.130, noted by Jump, "The Anonymous Masque," p. 190).

107

674. Fortune's blind side: Fortune was sometimes shown as bifrontal, often with one face fair and young, the other old and hideous. She is also at times depicted as blind or wearing a blindfold. A source may exist for the dramatist's combination of the two, but I have not located it.

681–682. An allusion to the figure of Occasion (also called Opportunity) who has a forelock in the front and is bald behind. She is often identified with Fortune or with Time. Cf. "Occasion is bald; take her by the forelock" (Chapman, *May Day*, 3.3.118).

s.d. 723–724. fancies: "This craze for odd bows of ribbon in [men's] hair . . . remained fashionable for about thirty years, in fact until the periwig took the place of natural hair." Cavalier tendencies (1640–1650) were indicated by wearing bows of ribbon (fancies) on one's lovelocks. Brooke, *English Costume*, pp. 40–42.

724–725. Age's song appears in four song collections of the 1650's (see Cyrus Lawrence Day and Eleanore Boswell Murrie, *English Song-Books, 1651–1702* and in James Shirley's first play, *The School of Complement*, acted in 1624 and printed in 1631 and 1637. The following is the first verse of this "amorous pastoral," as the song is called in Shirley's play:

> Turn, Amaryllis, to thy swain,
> Thy Damon calls thee back again;
> Here is a pretty arbour by,
> Where Apollo cannot pry,
> Here let's sit, and while I play,
> Sing to my pipe a roundelay.   [3.5]

See *The Dramatic Works and Poems of James Shirley*, ed. William Gifford and Alexander Dyce, I.

729–731. Cf. "Is this no small servitude for an enamorate to be every hour combing his head, stiffening his beard, perfuming his hair, washing his face, with sweet waters, painting, curling, and not to come abroad but sprucely crowned, decked, and apparelled?" (Burton, *Anatomy*, III, 161).

732–733. Cloris, Lesbia, Licoris: All three girls' names appear

108

frequently in seventeenth-century ballads. Lesbia is the name under which Catullus praised his lover Clodia; Licoris appears in Sannazzaro's eclogues; Cloris (cf. Jonson's *Chloridia*), as goddess of the flowers and associated with Zephrus, is similar to Flora.

738. Cf. "But for an old fool to dote, to see an old lecher, what more odious, what can be more absurd" (Burton, *Anatomy*, III, 56).

740–751. I have not been able to locate this song. It is probably original, since the dramatist tends to give only a line or two of reference to popular songs.

749. warble: to sing softly and sweetly in a birdlike manner (*OED*). Cf. "Come, warble, come" (*As You Like It*, 2.5.38).

760. foot: servant, toady. Possibly a pun on the French *foutre*.

785. satyrs: See the Introduction, p. 26. In Jonson's *Oberon*, the satyrs "despite their eternal impulse to kick over the traces, venerate and pay homage to the Fairy Prince. . . . Thus Jonson, in imaging control of misrule and its corollary the acceptance of rule, reflects a major theme of the speeches and songs praising King James as an ideal ruler" (Ben Jonson, "*Oberon*," ed. Richard Hosley, in *A Book of Masques*, ed. Gerald Eades Bentley, pp. 50–51).

793–794, satyrs' dance: The dance may have been a brawl or a brame. See Walter Sorrell, "Shakespeare and the Dance," *Shakespeare Quarterly* 7 (1947): 380. Satyrs' dances are generally "antic" dances; they perform "long handsprings and large leaps . . . full of gesture and swift motion" (Raffé, *Dictionary of the Dance*).

835–885. The purgation of Time is similar to an exorcism of demons. Several references are made to his being bewitched (see lines 366–369, 380, 392, 394, 433, 441, for example). The demon of a possessed subject occasionally solidifies itself into filth, excrement, intestinal rumblings, and vomit, in which form it is issued forth. See Emile Grillot de Givry, *Witchcraft, Magic and Alchemy*, pp. 157ff.

844–845. pun on "cross": (1) angry, (2) thwart. Love says that Juno should not cross Time's path because he is bewitched (witches are often splayfooted and have bad breath).

847. barking libels: See the Introduction, p. 9.

109

853–854. herbe of grace: rue. "The many good properties where unto Rue serveth hath, I think, in former times caused the English name of Herbe Grace to be given unto it. For without doubt it is a most wholesome herb, although bitter and strong . . ." (John Parkinson, *Paradise in Sole: Paradisus Terrestris* [1629], quoted from Esther Singleton, *The Shakespeare Garden* [New York: The Century Company, 1922], p. 229). A frequent pun, rue is connected with repentance, which is the chief sign of grace.

855. Proverbial: "Bitter pills may have blessed effects." Cf. "'Tis a physic / That's bitter to sweet end" (*Measure for Measure*, 4.4.8).

859–860. glister: variant of clyster, treatment with a medicine injected into the rectum; an injection, enema; sometimes a suppository. Shirley, *Bird in a Cage* (1633) 1.1: "He's a slight physician cannot give a golden glister at a dead lift" (*OED*).

881–882. swearing oaths, diurnals, weekly intelligences: See the Introduction, pp. 9–10.

900. enlarge: release.

927. See the note to line 227.

947–948. Cf. these lines from *I Henry VI*, 5.5.62:

> For what is wedlock forced, but a hell,
> An age of discord and continual strife?
> Whereas the contrary bringeth bliss,
> And is a pattern of celestial peace.

957. portion: dowry; "these" refers to Love's bow and quiver.

981. motions: an inward prompting or impulse; emotions (*OED*).

992. sick: fickle. Cf. "his broken wings full of sick feathers" (Chapman, *An Invective*, in *Poems*, p. 434ᵃ, quoted by Jump, "The Anonymous Masque," p. 190).

1010. To these things, also, God has given an end.

Byron's Tragedy

[Actus II A *Room in the Court*]

Enter Epernon, Soissons, Vitry, Pralin, *etc.* [*to the* King]

Ep. Will't please your Majesty to take your place? The Masque is coming.

Hen.　　Room, my lords; stand close.

Music and a song above, and Cupid *enters with a table written hung about his neck; after him two torch-bearers; after them* Marie, D'Entragues, *and four ladies more with their torch-bearers, etc.* Cupid *speaks.*

Cup. My lord, these nymphs, part of the scatter'd train
Of friendless Virtue (living in the woods
Of shady Arden, and of late not hearing　　　　　　　5
The dreadful sounds of war, but that sweet Peace,
Was by your valour lifted from her grave,
Set on your royal right hand, and all Virtues
Summon'd with honour and with rich rewards
To be her handmaids): these, I say, the Virtues　　　10
Have put their heads out of their caves and coverts,
To be your true attendants in your Court:
In which desire I must relate a tale
Of kind and worthy emulation
'Twixt these two Virtues, leaders of the train,　　　15
This on the right hand is Sophrosyne,
Or Chastity, this other Dapsile,

Reprinted from George Chapman, *The Conspiracy and Tragedy of Charles Duke of Byron*, in *The Plays of George Chapman: The Tragedies*, ed. Thomas Marc Parrott (London: Routledge & Kegan Paul Ltd., 1910; reprinted New York: Russell & Russell, 1961), by permission of Russell & Russell, Publishers.

Or Liberality; their emulation
Begat a jar, which thus was reconcil'd.
I (having left my Goddess mother's lap,   20
To hawk and shoot at birds in Arden groves)
Beheld this princely nymph with much affection,
Left killing birds, and turn'd into a bird,
Like which I flew between her ivory breasts
As if I had been driven by some hawk   25
To sue to her for safety of my life;
She smil'd at first, and sweetly shadow'd me
With soft protection of her silver hand;
Sometimes she tied my legs in her rich hair,
And made me (past my nature, liberty)   30
Proud of my fetters. As I pertly sat,
On the white pillows of her naked breasts,
I sung for joy; she answer'd note for note,
Relish for relish, with such ease and art
In her divine division, that my tunes   35
Show'd like the God of shepherds' to the Sun's,
Compar'd with hers; asham'd of which disgrace,
I took my true shape, bow, and all my shafts,
And lighted all my torches at her eyes;
Which set about her in a golden ring,   40
I follow'd birds again from tree to tree,
Kill'd and presented, and she kindly took.
But when she handled my triumphant bow,
And saw the beauty of my golden shafts,
She begg'd them of me; I, poor boy, replied   45
I had no other riches, yet was pleas'd
To hazard all and stake them gainst a kiss
At an old game I us'd, call'd penny-prick.
She, privy to her own skill in the play,
Answer'd my challenge; so I lost my arms,   50
And now my shafts are headed with her looks;
One of which shafts she put into my bow,
And shot at this fair nymph, with whom before,

I told your Majesty she had some jar.
The nymph did instantly repent all parts   55
She play'd in urging that effeminate war,
Lov'd and submitted; which submission
This took so well that now they both are one;
And as for your dear love their discords grew,
So for your love they did their loves renew.   60
And now to prove them capable of your Court
In skill of such conceits and qualities
As here are practis'd, they will first submit
Their grace in dancing to your Highness' doom,
And p[r]ay the press to give their measures room.   65
        Music, dance, etc., which done Cupid *speaks*
If this suffice for one Court compliment
To make them gracious and entertain'd,
Behold another parcel of their courtship,
Which is a rare dexterity in riddles,
Shown in one instance, which is here inscrib'd.   70
Here is a riddle, which if any knight
At first sight can resolve, he shall enjoy
This jewel here annex'd; which, though it show
To vulgar eyes no richer than a pebble,
And that no lapidary nor great man   75
Will give a sou for it, 'tis worth a kingdom;
For 'tis an artificial stone compos'd
By their great mistress, Virtue, and will make
Him that shall wear it live with any little
Suffic'd and more content than any king.   80
If he that undertakes cannot resolve it,
And that these nymphs can have no harbour here
(It being consider'd that so many Virtues
Can never live in Court), he shall resolve
To leave the Court and live with them in Arden.   85
    Ep.   Pronounce the riddle; I will undertake it.
    Cup.   'Tis this, sir.
What's that a fair lady most of all likes,

113

Yet ever makes show she least of all seeks:
That's ever embrac'd and affected by her,
Yet never is seen to please or come nigh her: 90
Most serv'd in her night-weeds, does her good in a corner:
But a poor man's thing, yet doth richly adorn her:
Most cheap and most dear, above all worldly pelf,
That is hard to get in, but comes out of itself:

   Ep.   Let me peruse it, Cupid.   95
   Cup.   Here it is.
   Ep.   Your riddle is good fame.
   Cup.   Good fame? How make you that good?
   Ep.   Good fame is that a good lady most likes, I am sure.
   Cup.   That's granted.   100
   Ep.   'Yet ever makes show she least of all seeks': for
she likes it only for virtue, which is not glorious.
   Hen.   That holds well.
   Ep.   'Tis 'ever embrac'd and affected by her', for she
must persevere in virtue or fame vanishes; 'yet never is   105
seen to please or come nigh her', for fame is invisible.
   Cup.   Exceeding right!
   Ep.   'Most served in her night-weeds', for ladies that
most wear their night-weeds come least abroad, and they
that come least abroad serve fame most, according to this: 110
Non forma, sed fama, in publicum exire debet.
   Hen.   'Tis very substantial.
   Ep.   'Does her good in a corner'—that is, in her most
retreat from the world comforts her; 'but a poor man's
thing': for every poor man may purchase it, 'yet doth   115
richly adorn' a lady.
   Cup.   That all must grant.
   Ep.   'Most cheap', for it costs nothing; 'and most dear'
for gold cannot buy it; 'above all worldly pelf', for that's
transitory, and fame eternal. 'It is hard to get in';   120
that is, hard to get; 'but comes out of itself', for when
it is virtuously deserved with the most inward retreat from

the world, it comes out in spite of it. And so, Cupid, your
jewel is mine.

    Cup.   It is: and be the virtue of it yours.
We'll now turn to our dance, and then attend   125
Your Highness' will, as touching our resort,
If Virtue may be entertain'd in Court.

    Hen.   This show hath pleased me well for that it figures
The reconcilement of my Queen and mistress:
Come, let us in and thank them, and prepare   130
To entertain our trusty friend Byron.   *Exeunt*

Finis Actus Secundi

References

Allen, John William. *English Political Thought*. London: Methuen & Co., 1938.

Bayne, Ronald. "Masque and Pastoral." In *The Cambridge History of English Literature*, vol. 6. Edited by A. W. Ward and A. R. Waller. Cambridge: Cambridge University Press, 1910.

Beaumont, Francis, and John Fletcher. *The Works of Francis Beaumont and John Fletcher*. Edited by Arnold Glover and A. R. Waller. 10 vols. Cambridge: Cambridge University Press, 1905–1912.

Bentley, Gerald Eades, ed. *A Book of Masques in Honour of Allardyce Nicoll*. Cambridge: Cambridge University Press, 1967.

Boas, Frederick Samuel. *Shakespeare and the Universities and Other Studies in Elizabethan Drama*. Oxford: B. Blackwell, 1923.

Brooke, Iris. *English Costume of the Seventeenth Century*. London: A. & C. Black, 1934.

Bullen, Arthur Henry. *A Collection of Old English Plays*. 4 vols. London: Wyman & Sons, 1882–1885.

Burton, Robert. *The Anatomy of Melancholy*. 3 vols. London: J. M. Dent & Sons, 1964.

Carew, Thomas. *The Poems of Thomas Carew*. Edited by Rhodes Dunlap. Oxford: Clarendon Press, 1949.

Chapman, George. *The Plays of George Chapman*. Edited by Thomas Marc Parrott. 4 vols. New York: Russell & Russell, 1961.

———. *The Poems of George Chapman*. Edited by Phyllis Brooks Bartlett. New York: Modern Language Association of America, 1941.

Chappell, William. *Popular Music of the Olden Time*. 2 vols. London: Cramer, Beale, & Chappell, 1859.

Chew, Samuel C. *The Pilgrimage of Life*. New Haven: Yale University Press, 1962.

Clarendon, Edward, Earl of. *The History of the Rebellion and Civil Wars in England*. Edited by W. Dunn Macray. 7 vols. Oxford: Clarendon Press, 1888.

116

Clarke, John. *Paroemiologia Anglo-Latina in Usum Scholarum Concinnata.* London: F. Kyngston for R. Mylbourne, 1639.

Cunnington, C. Willett, and Phillis Cunnington. *Handbook of English Costume in the Seventeenth Century.* London: Faber & Faber, 1955.

Cunnington, Phillis. *Costume in Pictures.* London: Studio Vista, 1964.

Cutts, John P. *La Musique de Scène de la Troupe de Shakespeare.* Paris: Gap, Éditions du Centre National de la Recherche Scientifique, 1959.

Dawson, Giles E., and Laetitia Kennedy-Skipton. *Elizabethan Handwriting, 1500–1650.* New York: W. W. Norton & Co., 1966.

Day, Cyrus Lawrence, and Eleanore Boswell Murrie. *English Song-Books, 1651–1702.* London: Printed for the Bibliographical Society at the University Press, Oxford, 1940.

Dekker, Thomas. *The Dramatic Works of Thomas Dekker.* Edited by R. H. Shepherd. 4 vols. London: J. Pearson, 1873.

Empson, William. *Some Versions of Pastoral.* London: Chatto & Windus, 1935.

Evelyn, John. *The Diary of John Evelyn.* Edited by E. S. de Beer. 6 vols. Oxford: Clarendon Press, 1955.

Ford, John. *The Works of John Ford.* Edited by William Gifford and Alexander Dyce. London: J. Toovey, 1869.

Frye, Northrop. *The Anatomy of Criticism.* Princeton, N.J.: Princeton University Press, 1957.

Furniss, W. Todd. "Ben Jonson's Masques." In *Three Studies in the Renaissance.* New Haven: Yale University Press, 1958.

Gombosi, Otto. "Some Musical Aspects of the English Court Masque," *Journal of the American Musicological Society* 1, no. 3 (1948): 3–19.

Greg, Walter W. *Pastoral Poetry and Pastoral Drama.* London: A. H. Bullen, 1906.

Grillot de Givry, Émile Angelo. *Witchcraft, Magic & Alchemy.* Translated by Courtenay Locke. New York: Houghton Mifflin Company, 1954.

Harbage, Alfred. *Cavalier Drama.* London: Oxford University Press, 1936.

———. "An Unnoted Caroline Dramatist," *Studies in Philology* 31 (1935). 28–36.

———, and S. Schoenbaum. *Annals of English Drama, 975–1700.* Philadelphia: University of Pennsylvania Press, 1940.

Hart, Arthur Tindal. *The Country Clergy in Elizabethan and Stuart Times, 1558–1660.* London: Phoenix House, 1958.

117

Horst, Louis. *Pre-Classic Dance Forms*. New York: The Dance Observer, 1940.

Hotson, Leslie. *The Commonwealth and Restoration Stage*. New York: Russell & Russell, 1962.

Hough, Graham. *A Preface to the Faerie Queene*. New York: W. W. Norton & Co., 1963.

James, Margaret. *Social Problems and Policy During the Puritan Revolution, 1640–1660*. New York: Barnes & Noble, 1967.

Jameson, Storm. *The Decline of Merry England*. New York: Bobbs-Merrill Co., 1930.

Jonson, Ben. *The Works of Ben Jonson*. Edited by C. H. Herford and Percy Simpson. 11 vols. Oxford: Oxford University Press, 1925–1953.

Jump, J. D. "The Anonymous Masque in MS. Egerton 1994," *Review of English Studies* 2 (April, 1935): 186–191.

Nichols, John. *Progresses of James I*. 4 vols. London: J. B. Nichols & Son, 1828.

Orgel, Stephen. *The Jonsonian Masque*. Cambridge, Mass.: Harvard University Press, 1965.

————. "To Make Boards to Speak: Inigo Jones' Stage and the Jonsonian Masque," *Renaissance Drama*, n.s. 1 (1968): 121–152.

Panofsky, Erwin. *Studies in Iconology*. New York: Harper & Row, 1962.

Playford, John. *The English Dancing Master*. London: [Published by] J. P[layford]., 1651.

The Roxburghe Ballads. Hertford: S. Austin & Sons, 1874.

Sabol, Andrew J. *Songs and Dances for the Stuart Masque*. Providence, R.I.: Brown University Press, 1959.

Schofield, Bertram, ed. *The Knyvett Letters, 1620–1644*. London: Constable & Co., 1950.

Shirley, James. *The Dramatic Works and Poems of James Shirley*. Edited by William Gifford and Alexander Dyce. 6 vols. New York: Russell & Russell, 1966, reprint of 1833 edition.

Siebert, F. S. *Freedom of the Press in England, 1476–1776*. Urbana: University of Illinois Press, 1952.

Smith, Hallett. *Elizabethan Poetry*. Cambridge, Mass.: Harvard University Press, 1952.

Sorrell, Walter. "Shakespeare and the Dance," *Shakespeare Quarterly* 8 (1957): 366–384.

Spivack, Charlotte. *George Chapman*. New York: Twayne Publishers, 1967.

Taylor, John. *The Works of John Taylor.* Publications of the Spenser Society, no. 7. First Collection. Manchester: C. S. Simms, 1870.

Wakeman, H. O. *The Church and the Puritans, 1570–1660.* London: Longmans, Green & Co., 1894.

Wedgwood, Cicely Veronica. *The King's War.* London: Collins, 1958.

Westmorland, Mildmay Fane, Earl of. *Mildmay Fane's "Raguaillo d'Oceano," 1640, and "Candy Restored," 1641.* Ed. Clifford Leech. Louvain: Librairie Universitaire, 1938.

Wither, George. *Juvenalia.* Publications of the Spenser Society, nos. 9–11. Manchester: C. S. Simms, 1871.

White, Helen C., Ruth C. Wallerstein, and Ricardo Quintana, eds. *Seventeenth Century Verse and Prose*, vol. 1, *1600–1660.* New York: Macmillan Co., 1964.